What does the chimpanzee eat in its natural habitat?

Which alphabet is the most widely used in the world?

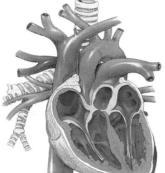

Where is this organ in the body and what does it pump?

In heraldry, where might you find a charge on a field?

Which famous cycling race, lasting 26 days, takes place in France?

Which country has 20 sheep for every human?

Clowns are sometimes called "Joey." How did they get this nickname?

For 700 years, samurai dominated Japan. Who were they?

What color would a pair of red shoes appear in blue light?

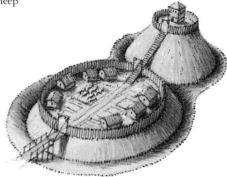

What kind of castle is this and when was it built?

What does this instrument record?

How does the deadly black widow spider get its name?

Why is the arrow-poison frog so brightly colored?

In ancient Greece, what were the Spartans famous for?

What kind of musical instrument is this?

THE DORLING KINDERSLEY
Question & Answer
Quiz Book

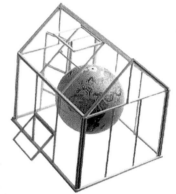

How is carbon dioxide contributing to the warming of our globe?

Written by
ANN KRAMER & THEODORE ROWLAND-ENTWISTLE

On which island off the east coast of Africa does this animal live?

What is this structure called and where would you see it?

What is this theater called and when was it built?

DORLING KINDERSLEY
London • New York • Stuttgart

Can you name this modern building, and say what it is used for?

A DORLING KINDERSLEY BOOK

Project Editor
Liza Bruml
Art Editor
Sarah Scrutton
U.S. Editor
B. Alison Weir
Managing Editor
Simon Adams
Managing Art Editor
Julia Harris
Picture Research
Fergus Muir and Charlotte Bush
Production
Catherine Semark

First American Edition, 1994
10 9 8 7 6 5 4 3 2 1

Published in the United States by
Dorling Kindersley Publishing, Inc., 95 Madison Avenue
New York, New York 10016

Library of Congress Cataloging-in-Publication Data
Kramer, Ann.
    The Dorling Kindersley question and answer quiz book / by Ann
Kramer & Theodore Rowland-Entwistle.
       p.   cm.
    Includes index.
    ISBN 1-56458-678-2
    1. Children's questions and answers.   2. Curiosities and wonders–
–Juvenile literature.   I. Rowland-Entwistle. Theodore. II. Title.
AG195.K73   1994
031.02--dc20
                                        94-20135
                                          CIP
                                          AC

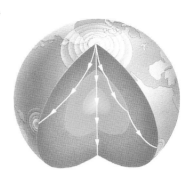

Color reproduction by Colourscan, Singapore
Printed and bound in Italy by A. Mondadori Editore, Verona

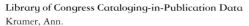

Contents

Test yourself on people and places

Windmill

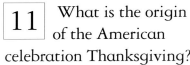

Thanksgiving supper

1 What is the name of the kind of government where there is "rule by the people"?

2 Why are windmills a common sight in the Netherlands?

3 Which single country produces about one fifth of the world's wine?
Grape harvesting

4 What is a stupa, and with which religion is it associated?

Painted egg faces

5 Sometimes a clown in a circus is called "Joey." Where did this nickname come from?

6 Which vast region in the Russian Federation stretches from the Ural Mountains to Alaska?

7 Where might you find Tuareg, Ashanti, and Masai people?
Tuareg
Ashanti   Masai

8 What is karma, and why is it so important to Buddhists?
Sitting Buddha

9 What do the tabla, tambura, and sitar have in common?

10 Where was Parcheesi first played?

11 What is the origin of the American celebration Thanksgiving?

12 Which Italian city was built on a small group of islands in a lagoon?

13 What is UNICEF and what does it do?

14 Can you name the canal that links the Mediterranean and Red seas?

15 Which city was specially built to replace Rio de Janeiro as the capital of Brazil?

16 Shiva, Vishnu, and Brahma are gods of which religion?

Vishnu   Brahma   Shiva

17 In which sport might you race for the America's Cup, and how did the winner's trophy get its name?

18 These national symbols represent which four countries?
Shamrock   Thistle   Leek   Rose

19 In an orchestra, what does the conductor use a small stick, called a baton, for?

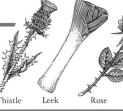

20 How did the cuddly teddy bear get its name?
Teddy bears

Test yourself on people and places

The Silk Road

Huskies pulling sled

21 What are the people who live in the Arctic called?

22 The Silk Road runs through Central Asia. What was it first used for?

23 Why do lots of tourists flock to the town of Oberammergau every ten years?

Intensive agriculture

24 Which is the most widely used alphabet in the world?

Diviner

25 Why does a dowser, or diviner, use a Y-shaped hazel or willow twig?

26 There are many kinds of puppets. What sort is a marionette?

The Koran

27 The Bible is sacred to both Jews and Christians. Which religion believes in the Koran?

28 In which religion do the men wear a shawl called a tallith and a skullcap called a yarmulke?

Boating on the lake

29 What is so special about Lake Titicaca?

30 The Japanese are proud of their traditional culture. What is their national sport?

Japanese flag

31 Some of the people of the modern state of Israel live on kibbutzim. What is unusual about the kibbutz way of life?

32 What is the difference between intensive and subsistence farming?

33 Scandinavia, in northern Europe, is made up of which countries?

34 Indonesia consists of thousands of islands. Where is its capital?

35 Which nation has 20 times more sheep than people?

Sheep shearing

36 More than one-fifth of the world's population lives in just one country. Which one?

Processional dragon

37 Many people work on a movie set. What is the director responsible for?

38 Which is Europe's longest river, and where does it flow?

39 If guerillas are not a kind of ape, what are they?

TURN TO PAGES 12 AND 13 FOR THE ANSWERS

9

Answers for people and places quiz

1 Democracy. In this kind of government the people play a part, usually by voting for representatives to make decisions on their behalf.

Voting at a ballot box

2 Much of the land in the Netherlands is below sea level. To prevent flooding, barriers called dykes have been built. The water is then pumped from the enclosed areas, which are known as polders. Windmills were once used to power the pumps that drained the land.

3 France, the largest country in western Europe. It has many very famous wine-growing regions, including Bordeaux, Burgundy, and Champagne. France is also well-known for its good food, particularly cheeses such as Brie and Camembert, and goat's cheese.

French flag

4 A stupa is a dome-shaped mound of brick or stone covering a site or object sacred to Buddha. Many stupas are found in India, the birthplace of Buddhism about 2,500 years ago.

Indian stupa

5 Clowns take their nickname, and their white faces, from the Englishman Joseph Grimaldi (1779-1837). With his painted face, he is considered to be the first real stage clown.

Joseph Grimaldi

6 Siberia. Much of northern Siberia lies inside the Arctic Circle. Most of the population live close to the Trans-Siberian Railway, which runs from Moscow to Vladivostok.

Sunset in Siberia

7 In the African continent. The Tuareg are Muslim nomads who inhabit the Sahara. Ashantis live in the dense forests of West Africa. The tall Masai people herd cattle on the open plains of Kenya.

Africa

Buddhist wheel of life

8 Buddhists believe that everyone is reborn. They think that karma, or the sum of good and bad deeds that a person did in one life, will affect the quality of their next life.

9 They are all traditional Indian musical instruments. The tabla is a drum; the sitar and tambura are stringed. The musicians improvise melodies that are based on ragas — a fixed series of notes.

Tambura

Sitar

Tabla

10 The ancient board game of pachisi was first played in India, and is still the national game. The modern version, called Parcheesi, is based on its Indian predecessor.

Parcheesi

Answers for people and places quiz

11 In November 1621, the English settlers in North America held a thanksgiving feast to celebrate their first harvest. Every year Thanksgiving Day is repeated on the fourth Thursday in November.

Venice, Italy

12 Venice, a beautiful city built on 118 islands. It is linked to the mainland by a causeway, but most people travel by gondola or motorboat on the network of canals.

13 UNICEF is the United Nations Children's Fund. It was set up in 1946 by the United Nations to help child victims of World War II. The fund now provides medical help and education to children around the world.

UNICEF symbol

14 The Suez Canal, a major waterway and trade route that was completed in 1869. Cutting through the Isthmus of Suez to link the two seas, it reduces the sailing distance around the world.

Suez Canal

15 Brasilia. In 1960, it was made the seat of government and the capital of Brazil. The city was designed in the shape of an aircraft, and its futuristic architecture contrasts with its rural surroundings.

Brasilia

16 Shiva the destroyer, Vishnu the preserver, and Brahma the creator are the three most important gods of the Hindu religion. One of the world's oldest religions, Hinduism began in India more than 5,000 years ago.

Hindu "Om" symbol

17 Ocean racing. Two yachts from different nations race a triangular course. The trophy is named after the first winner of the race, the U.S. yacht *America*.

Sailing

18 The shamrock is the national emblem of Ireland, the thistle belongs to Scotland, the leek is the national emblem of Wales, and the rose is England's national flower. Scotland, Wales, England, and Northern Ireland make up the United Kingdom. Its flag is the Union Jack.

Union Jack

19 Some orchestras may contain as many as 90 musicians. To make sure they keep time, the conductor uses a baton or hand motions to give the orchestra the correct tempo, or speed. The conductor also interprets the composer's music.

Conductor with his baton

20 The teddy bear is said to have been named after U.S. president Theodore Roosevelt, whose nickname was Teddy. In 1902, on a hunting trip, Roosevelt refused to kill a bear cub. Later, a shopkeeper began selling toy bears, calling them teddy bears.

Answers for people and places quiz

Inuit hunt seal to eat

21 Inuit, which means "real men." The name "Eskimo", means "eaters of meat," and was given to the Inuit by Native North Americans.

26 A marionette is a string puppet. It is worked from above by tilting a bar, which pulls the strings. This moves the puppet's arms, legs, and head.

String puppets

22 From the 1st century BC until the development of a sea route in the 1600s, traders and merchants traveled the perilous Silk Road to bring silks and other precious goods from China to Europe.

Camels are led along the route

27 The followers of the religion Islam, who are called Muslims (or Moslems), read the Koran, which is the holy book of Islam. Muslims believe it is the direct word of God, or Allah, as revealed to his prophet, Muhammad. The Koran consists of 114 *suras*, or chapters, that are written in verse.

23 Every ten years the inhabitants of Oberammergau in Germany reenact Jesus Christ's crucifixion. Visitors come from all over the country and abroad to see the passion play performances.

Passion play

28 The tallith, a shawl worn by men during prayers, and the yarmulke, or kipa, are both used in Judaism, the Jewish religion.

Menorah

Yarmulke

Tallith

Torah

24 All western languages, as well as the written languages of Africa, are based on the Roman alphabet, which was developed in about the 7th century BC. Then it had only 21 letters; J, U, W, Y, and Z were added later.

Roman letters in alphabetic order

29 High in the Andes mountains, 12,507 ft (3,812 m) above sea level, Lake Titicaca is the world's highest navigable lake. It lies between Bolivia and Peru, covering an area of about 3,200 sq miles (8,300 sq km). Both ships and traditional reed boats use the lake.

South America

25 Dowsing is an ancient way of finding water. The dowser holds one end of the Y-shaped twig in each hand, and walks around until the stem twitches downward, showing where water is buried.

30 Sumo wrestling. In this sport the two contestants, who follow a special diet for strength and weight, try to push each other out of a small ring.

Sumo wrestlers

Answers for people and places quiz

Kibbutz inhabitants working together as a community on the farm

31 A kibbutz (which means "gathering") is a special kind of farm. The people who live on these farms are all equal. They work together, sharing the land, food, and decision making. The children are brought up collectively.

Intensive chicken houses

Subsistence farming

32 Intensive farming produces surpluses of crops and livestock for a farmer to sell for profit. Subsistence farming produces only just enough produce for a farmer to live on.

33 Historically the region known as Scandinavia consisted of Norway and Sweden. Today, it also includes other places where Nordic people live. Denmark, Finland, and Iceland are now considered part of Scandinavia as is Greenland.

Scandinavia

34 Indonesia's many islands straddle the equator from Malaysia to Australia. Most Indonesians live on the island of Java, which is also the site of the country's capital, Jakarta.

Borobudur, Java

35 New Zealand. With its warm, moist climate, the country is ideal for farming, especially sheep and cattle. New Zealand is the world's leading exporter of lamb and dairy produce, and is the second largest exporter of wool.

New Zealand flag

36 China. This vast country is the third largest in the world. More than a billion people live in China, which makes it the most populated country in the world.

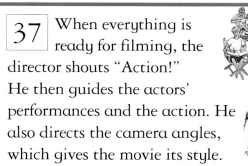

The family is very important in the Chinese way of life

37 When everything is ready for filming, the director shouts "Action!" He then guides the actors' performances and the action. He also directs the camera angles, which gives the movie its style.

Movie set

38 Europe's longest river is the Volga River, which flows 2,290 miles (3,688 km) through Russia from the Valdai Hills to the Caspian Sea. Boats use it to transport goods across the country.

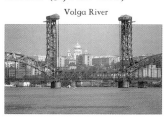

Volga River

39 Named after the Spanish for "little war," guerrillas are fighters who are not regular soldiers. Working in small groups, guerrillas make sudden raids on invading forces.

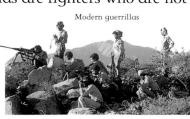

Modern guerrillas

The amazing world of buildings

Q In which colossal theater did gladiators fight wild animals?

Elevator lifted animals into the arena

A Nearly 2,000 years ago in ancient Rome, spectators flocked to the Colosseum to watch public "games" featuring fights between hungry animals and human gladiators, chariot races, and mock battles.

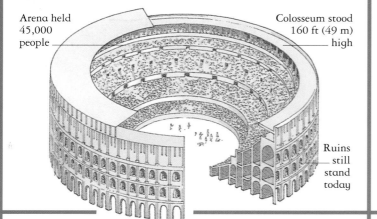

Arena held 45,000 people

Colosseum stood 160 ft (49 m) high

Ruins still stand today

Q Where in Spain might you find a fantastic, unfinished Holy Family?

A The fantastic wrought-iron spires of the cathedral of Sagrada Familia, or Holy Family, are among the most famous sights in Barcelona. Designed by the great Catalan architect Antonio Gaudi (1852-1926), work began on the cathedral in 1882 but is still unfinished today.

Spires reach high into the sky

Q This famous modern English building has its insides on the outside. What is its name, and who occupies it?

A In 1986 the famous insurance company Lloyds of London moved to new offices – the Lloyds Building. It was designed by the British architect Richard Rogers. The appearance of the building caused much argument because all its internal services, such as the plumbing, are on the outside.

Q Which spectacular Indian temple was built for the love of a woman?

A Covered with marble and inlaid with semiprecious stones, the Taj Mahal is one of the world's most beautiful buildings. It was built by the Mogul emperor, Shah Jahan, in memory of his wife, Mumtaz Mahal, who died in 1631.

Towers are called minarets

Magnificent natural wonders

Q Why are the Himalayas sometimes known as the "roof of the world"?

A With their rugged peaks and valleys, the mighty Himalayas form the highest mountain range in the world. They lie on the border between China and Nepal. The range includes Mount Everest, which, at 29,028 ft (8,848 m), is the world's tallest mountain.

The summit of Everest was first reached by E. Hillary and T. Norgay in 1953

Q Where in Arizona might you ride a mule through years and years of history?

A Northwestern Arizona is home to the spectacular Grand Canyon. Carved out by the Colorado River, the eroded rock represents millions of years of the Earth's history. The canyon is 18 miles (29 km) wide in places, and more than 6,000 ft (1,820 m) deep. Tourists can ride down, past layers of geological history, to the very bottom.

Q How did Monument Valley, in Arizona and Utah, get its name?

A This arid wilderness in the American Southwest is famous for its remarkable columns of rock. These tall sandstone structures look like monuments.

Extraordinary shapes have been formed by wind-borne sand

Q At what time of day does Ayers Rock in central Australia change color?

Aboriginals

A Ayers Rock (Uluru) is a huge mass of sandstone, rising 1,142 ft (348 m) above a flat desert floor. It is sacred to the Aboriginals. Caves at the base are decorated with traditional Aboriginal paintings. At sunset, when rays from the setting sun strike the rock, it glows a deep red.

Sports facts

Q What is the origin of modern tennis?

A An indoor game known as royal tennis was first played in France about 800 years ago. The court had open windows, doors, and a sloping roof. It was not until the 19th century that tennis was played on grass.

Handle was designed to reduce wind resistance

Early lawn tennis racket

Modern racket is made from a combination of materials

Q Which famous cycling race, lasting 26 days, takes place in France?

A Every summer, some of the world's finest cyclists travel to France to take part in the Tour de France. It is an extremely grueling road race covering a course of about 2,200 miles (3,500 km). A yellow jersey is awarded to the overall leader at the end of each stage of the race.

Yellow jersey is worn by the overall leader of the race

Q When and where were the first Olympic Games held?

A The world's first Olympic Games began as a men-only religious festival at Olympia in ancient Greece, more than 2,000 years ago. There was only one race. More events were added later. The first modern Olympics were held in Athens, Greece, in 1896.

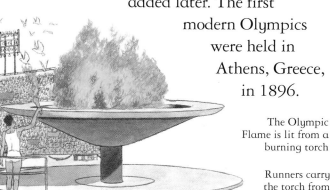

The Olympic Flame is lit from a burning torch

Runners carry the torch from Olympia to the site of the games

Cowboys skillfully lasso and bring down cattle

Q The word "rodeo" is from the Spanish word meaning "roundup." How did the sport of rodeo begin?

A In the American West many years ago, cattle roamed freely instead of being fenced in. Cowboys had to round up the cattle in spring and fall. During breaks, the cowboys often competed against one another at skills such as steer wrestling and calf roping. These competitions developed into the modern rodeo.

Remarkable cities of the world

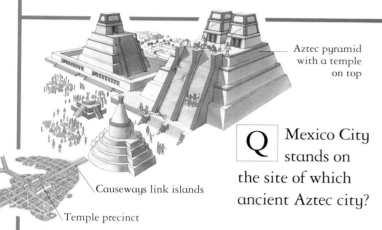

Aztec pyramid with a temple on top

Causeways link islands

Temple precinct

Q Mexico City stands on the site of which ancient Aztec city?

A The Aztecs, who ruled Mexico until 1519, founded a mighty empire. Their capital, Tenochtitlan, was a "floating city." It was built on islands in Lake Texcoco. Today Mexico City, the capital of Mexico, lies on the site of Tenochtitlan.

Mexico City is the most populated city in the world today

Q Which city-within-a-city is the smallest independent state in the world?

A Tucked inside Rome, the historic capital of Italy, is another city. Known as Vatican City and ruled by the Pope, it is the world's tiniest independent state. It covers an area of just 0.17 sq miles (0.44 sq km).

The Vatican is the center of the Roman Catholic Church

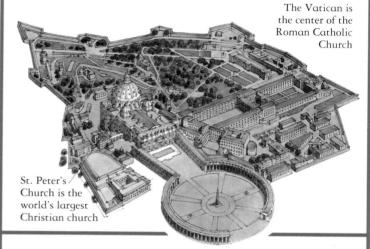

St. Peter's Church is the world's largest Christian church

Q The Brandenburg Gate stands on an east/west line that once divided which German city?

A After World War II, the German capital of Berlin was split in two. In 1989, the dividing wall was demolished and Berlin was reunited.

The Brandenburg Gate formed part of the wall that separated East and West Berlin

Berlin was reinstated as the capital of Germany in 1990

Q For the followers of which three great religions is Jerusalem holy?

A Every year millions of people flock to Jerusalem. Christians visit the Church of the Holy Sepulcher, where they believe Christ was buried. Jews pray at the Wailing Wall, the ruins of Herod's temple. Muslims worship at the Dome of the Rock Mosque, where they believe Muhammad ascended to heaven.

Jerusalem, Israel

Islamic star and moon

Christian cross

Jewish Star of David

Name these famous buildings

ANCIENT BUILDINGS
Here are two monuments and one temple. What are they called, and where in the world can you find them?

1

2

3

MODERN BUILDINGS
Can you name these 20th-century buildings and say what they are used for?

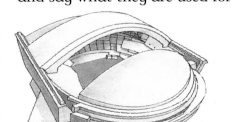

1

2

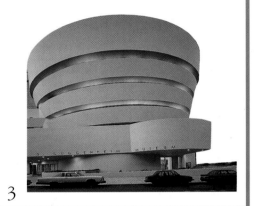

3

TALL STRUCTURES
What are the names of these six structures, where would you see them, and which one of them stands the tallest? Hint: They are not shown to scale.

1

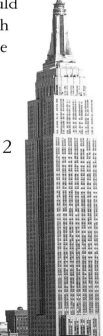

2

3

4

5

6

Find the picture that does not belong

Except for one picture, all the pictures in each of these boxes are linked in some way. Can you figure out the connection, and also find the picture in each box that does not belong?

ARTISTS

1

2

3

MUSICAL INSTRUMENTS

1

2

3

FLAGS

1

2

3

SPORTS

1

2

3

4

UNIFORMS

1

2

3

4

BUILDINGS

1

2

3

4

TURN TO PAGE 64 FOR THE ANSWERS

Test yourself on nature

1 Swimming in the sea, why would you avoid a Portuguese man-of-war?

Portuguese man-of-war

2 Why is the arrow-poison frog that lives in rain forests so brightly colored?

Arrow-poison frog

3 Which huge, flightless bird lays the world's largest egg?

Huge egg and hen's egg

4 Smooth and skeletal muscles are both found in the human body. How do they differ from each other?

5 Over short distances, which animal can run at about 60 mph (100 km/h) – as fast as a car?

Adult horse

6 A sett is an underground system of tunnels. Which nocturnal animal lives in this kind of home, and how is it built?

7 Cows are often seen lying down chewing the cud. What is cud, and why do they chew it?

8 How are the pearls that come from oysters and some other shellfish made?

Blister pearl

9 Inside which sea mammal would you find spermaceti oil?

10 Why do beavers spend their time cutting down trees?

Beaver gnaws at tree

11 What is a mermaid's purse, and where would you find one?

Mermaid

12 Bacon and ham come from which farm animal?

13 What are the three kinds of blood cells found in the human body, and what are their jobs?

14 A lizard sometimes sheds its tail. When might it do this, and what happens to the tail?

Tailless tree skunk

15 Can you name the three main types of horses, and say which type is the smallest?

16 Where would you find anthers, stigmas, and styles?

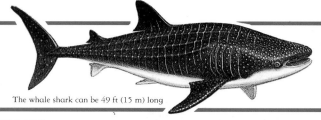

The whale shark can be 49 ft (15 m) long

17 The whale shark is the biggest fish, but there are other larger creatures living in the sea. What is the largest sea creature?

18 There are about 40 cacao beans in every pod, or fruit, of the cacao tree. What are the beans used for?

19 Why was the marine toad taken to Australia in the 1930s?

Marine toad

Test yourself on nature

20 The common flea jumps onto people to bite them. How far is it able to leap?

Flea gets airborne

21 Why does a dog sometimes hang its tongue out of its mouth and pant?

Panting dog

22 Can flying squirrels and flying lemurs really fly through the air?

Flying squirrel

23 Fossils of ammonites are some of the most commonly found stony remains. What were ammonites?

24 Why do leafcutter ants march back to their nest carrying bits of leaf?

Ants bite off huge pieces of leaf

25 Why are the boa snakes of tropical America and the pythons of Africa, Asia, and Australia known as "constrictors"?

26 A dromedary camel has one hump and a Bactrian camel has two humps. What is in the hump (or humps)?

27 Why do some warm-blooded animals hibernate?

Hibernating dormouse

28 What kind of tree grows to be the tallest in the world?

29 Which dinosaur was the largest known meat-eating creature of all time?

30 Why do snakes stick out their tongues and flick them?

Pit viper

31 The mudskipper, unlike most other fish, can spend long periods out of water. How does it survive on land?

32 Crocodiles and alligators look very similar. How can you tell them apart?

33 When a honeybee "dances" in a figure eight, what is it telling other bees in the hive?

Figure–eight pattern

34 The coldest place on Earth is on the ice of the Antarctic. How do newborn emperor penguins survive in this cold?

35 How are the spiny anteater and the platypus different from other kinds of mammals?

Spiny anteater   *Platypus*

36 Bats are nighttime creatures. What special noises do they make to help them find their way in the dark?

37 What animal is the closest living land relative to the elephant?

African elephant

38 Which group of animals feed their young on milk?

39 Why do male grasshoppers and crickets make a chirping sound?

Chirping grasshopper

TURN TO PAGES 26 AND 27 FOR THE ANSWERS

23

Answers for nature quiz

1 The Portuguese man-of-war is a floating colony of hundreds of jellyfish-like creatures called polyps. Some of the polyps trail tentacles with stinging cells. If you touch a tentacle, you trigger one of these cells, which will then sting you with a poison.

2 The arrow-poison frog's skin contains poison. The bright colors of the skin, which include yellow, orange, blue, and red, warn predators that the frog is poisonous to eat.

3 The world's largest egg is laid by the ostrich, the world's biggest living bird. The egg is about 8 in (20 cm) tall and weighs 3 lb 8 oz (1.6 kg), 30 times as much as a hen's egg.

Ostrich with her chicks

4 Smooth muscle is found in your digestive system, bladder, and blood vessels. It works automatically, even when you are asleep. Skeletal, or striated, muscle is different because you can control it at will. It covers your bones and is used to move them.

Skeletal muscle

Smooth muscle

5 In a sprint the fastest land animal is the cheetah, a member of the cat family. Over a long distance the pronghorn antelope of North America holds the record.

Cheetah bounds after prey and then pounces

6 The badger, a member of the weasel family, lives in a sett. It uses its strong claws to build the tunnels of the sett in the side of a bank or among tree roots. Over the years more tunnels are added. A large sett may be 100 years old.

Badger

7 Cows eat grass, which has to be well chewed before it can be fully digested. The cow has four stomachs. Grass is stored in the first stomach and later brought up in a wad, the cud, which is chewed thoroughly and then passed to the other stomachs.

Cow has four stomachs

8 A pearl is created when a piece of grit lodges in the shell. The shellfish covers the grit with a layer of shell lining known as mother-of-pearl, or nacre. The pearl that is formed removes the irritating grit.

Irritating grit in shell

Nacre forms around grit

Pearl comes free from shell

9 Spermaceti oil is a waxy substance that fills the huge square forehead of the sperm whale. Scientists believe that it may help the whale keep its balance when deep diving.

Enormous sperm whale

10 A beaver uses branches to dam streams and to make its home, called a lodge. The lodge is built from sticks and mud in the pool of water formed by the dam. In the lodge the beaver hollows out a dry chamber above water level to live in. Beavers eat bark, twigs, and leaves.

24

Answers for nature quiz

11 A mermaid's purse is the case of eggs laid by a shark or ray. The fish lay their eggs near the seashore, anchored to seaweed or rocks by tendrils. After the eggs have hatched, the rubbery cases are often washed up onto the beach.

Egg cases

16 Anthers, stigmas, and styles are parts of a flower. The anthers contain pollen and are male flower parts. The stigmas, which receive the pollen, are held on styles and are female flower parts.

Stigma
Style
Anther

12 The pig. Pork is the name given to fresh pig meat. Bacon is pork that has been "cured" by treating it with salt, and sometimes smoking it. Ham, which also comes from the pig, is usually from the hind leg of the animal. It can be either smoked or cured.

Different types of meat come from the pig

17 The blue whale is not only the largest sea creature but also the largest animal that has ever lived. It grows to about 100 ft (30 m) long and weighs up to 134 tons (136 tonnes) – about as heavy as 2,000 people!

Blue whale

13 A tiny drop of blood contains about five million cells. Some are red cells, which carry oxygen around the body. Others are white cells, which fight infection. Platelets are the third kind of cell. They help make the blood clot.

Platelet
Red cell *White cell*

18 Cacao beans are roasted, shelled, and then ground into a paste called cocoa butter. Cocoa butter and sugar are the main ingredients of chocolate. Cocoa is an ancient mis-spelling of the Mayan word cacao.

Chocolate

14 The end of a lizard's tail breaks off if it is seized by a predator, such as a bird or a cat. The broken-off piece of tail twitches for a bit. This confuses the enemy while the lizard escapes. The lizard's tail will regrow in about eight months.

Tree skunk's tail has regrown

19 The marine toad was originally found only in Central and South America. In the 1930s it was taken to Australia to eat cane beetles, which are pests of the sugarcane crop. The toad bred so successfully that it is now a serious pest itself.

Australia

15 The three main types are draft horses, light horses, and ponies. Draft horses, such as Shires, are used to pull plows; light horses, such as Arabians, take part in races. The pony is the smallest type, less than 5 ft (1.5 m) high at the shoulder.

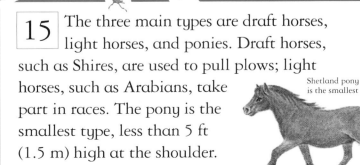

Shetland pony is the smallest

Appaloosa is a light horse

Shire is a draft horse

Answers for nature quiz

20 A common flea can jump more than 12 in (30 cm). That is the same as a person jumping 800 ft (245 m), which is higher than a 70-story building, or St. Paul's Cathedral in London, England.

Flea

St. Paul's

21 Unlike humans, dogs do not sweat through their skin to cool themselves. There are sweat glands on a dog's paw pads, but not much heat can be lost through the feet. To cool itself down quickly the dog pants, or breathes rapidly, to give off heat from its mouth and tongue.

22 Neither of these animals can really fly. They have no wings to flap so they cannot climb upward into the air under their own power. They can only swoop or glide, using their tails to steer.

Flying lemur

23 Ammonites were sea creatures with spiral shells, similar to the modern nautilus. They were common in prehistoric times but they died out, along with the dinosaurs, about 65 million years ago.

Fossil

24 Leafcutter ants feed on fungus. In their nest the ants chew the pieces of leaf they have cut. Then they mix the leaf with saliva to make a compost, on which the fungus grows.

25 These snakes are known as constrictors because they constrict, or squeeze, their prey. Instead of giving their prey a poisonous bite to kill it, they coil their bodies tightly around the victim until it is squeezed to death.

Emerald tree boa

26 A camel's hump stores reserves of fat. This fat allows it to travel for long periods across the desert without eating or drinking. It survives by living off the fatty fluid in its hump. The hump shrinks when the camel is hungry.

Dromedary camel

27 Animals hibernate – a sleeplike state – in a sheltered place to survive the cold winter months. Some desert animals, such as snails, have to "sleep" through summer to survive the intense heat. This is called estivation.

Estivating snails

28 A giant sequoia tree, which is named *General Sherman,* is the largest tree in the world. It grows in Sequoia National Park, California. It is over 270 ft (82 m) tall and its weight is estimated at 2,500 tons.

Giant sequoia

29 The ferocious *Tyrannosaurus rex* was the largest carnivorous dinosaur. It lived between 67 and 65 millions of years ago, so all the details known about this monster have come from its fossils.

Tyrannosarus rex was about 46 ft (14 m) long

Answers for nature quiz

30 Animals have to be aware of their surroundings to survive. A snake flicks out its tongue to detect odors in the air. The smells that stick to its wet tongue are tasted and help the snake to follow prey, find a mate, and avoid danger.

31 The mudskipper is able to leave the water and skip across mudflats and swamps using its fins as "legs." Like a diver with an Aqua-Lung, the mudskipper carries its air supply in the form of water kept in its large gill chambers.

Mudskippers clinging onto a reed

32 Look at their teeth! When its mouth is closed an alligator shows no teeth. But a crocodile always shows the fourth tooth on each side of its lower jaw. Both animals are meat eaters, and they use their teeth to grab prey.

Crocodile shows its tooth

Alligator shows no teeth

33 A honeybee dances the figure–eight pattern to inform other bees in the hive of the location, in relation to the sun, of a source of pollen or nectar.

Mother dog and suckling puppies

34 The male penguin keeps the eggs warm between his feet and belly. When the eggs hatch, the chicks stay warm by standing on their parents' feet to keep off the cold ice.

Emperor penguins

35 Unlike most mammals, the spiny anteater, or echidna, and the platypus lay eggs instead of giving birth to live young. When the eggs hatch, the mother feeds the babies on milk. These animals are known as monotremes, and they are both found in Australia.

36 Bats find their way – and their prey – by making very high-pitched squeaks and clicks. The sounds bounce back off nearby objects and are detected by the bat's large ears. This is called echolocation and gives the bat information about the object.

37 Believe it or not, it is the rock hyrax, which looks like a guinea pig and is about the size of a rabbit. Like the elephant, hyraxes are vegetarian, have long front teeth that grow throughout their lives, and have similar foot bones.

Small furry rock hyrax

38 The only creatures that feed their young with milk are mammals. The milk is produced in mammary glands on the chest or abdomen. The young babies suck the milk from the mother's teats.

39 The males chirp to attract a female or to warn off rival males. The noise is made by rubbing together the ridged veins on the front wings, or by rubbing the toothed ridge on the back leg against the wing vein.

Grasshopper

Ridged veins on wing

Toothed ridges on back leg

Strange creatures of the sea

Q What is unusual about the way in which sea horses breed?

A Unlike most living creatures, it is the male sea horse that gives birth. In the breeding season the female lays as many as 200 eggs in a special pouch on the front of the male's abdomen. The eggs develop in the pouch, and after about four weeks the baby sea horses are born.

Tail is used to hold on to the coral

Male rests after giving birth to baby sea horses

Q Why does the sand tiger shark never give birth to more than two young sharks at a time?

A There can be as many as 15 embryo sharks in a mother sand tiger shark's womb at first. But as the babies develop, they eat each other until there are just two left. The lucky survivors are born fully formed and are already ferocious creatures. They immediately leave their mother and swim away in search of other fish to eat.

Q In the depths of the sea, why is the viperfish such a fearsome hunter?

A The viperfish has a long, flexible spike on its back, which it uses like a fishing rod. When it hunts, it holds the spike over its head. Curious fish are attracted to the spike's glowing tip. Once lured, the viperfish uses its long fangs to stab its victim. The prey, trapped in the hunter's mouth by its curved teeth, is then swallowed whole.

Long spike

Curved teeth prevent the victim from escaping

Long fangs

Fin rays open in the air

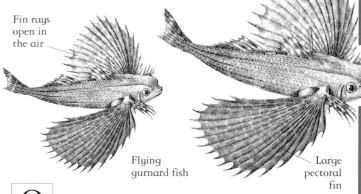

Flying gurnard fish

Large pectoral fin

Q Is it true that some fish can fly?

A No fish can actually fly. But some fish, called flying fish, can leap out of the water using their strong tails. Their pectoral fins act as "wings," helping them glide through the air. Out of water, flying fish look like giant dragonflies. When they swim they fold in their fins to make a streamlined shape.

Surprising feathery friends

Q Why does a cassowary have a bony helmet on its head?

A All three species of the cassowary bird live in the thick forests of Australasia. They are huge flightless birds that feed on fruits, berries, and seeds. The tall horny casque on its head is used to push aside the tangled forest undergrowth. The survival of these birds is threatened by the destruction of forests.

Horny casque

Two-wattled cassowary

Cassowary chick is reared by the male

Q Which tiny bird hums to stay still in midair?

A To stay in one place in the air, the hummingbird flaps its wings nonstop, just as a swimmer treads water to stay afloat. Its wings beat between 20 and 50 times a second to keep it hovering. This fast beating makes the humming sound you hear when the bird feeds from a flower.

Blades spin fast when the helicopter hovers

Q Which majestic bird is the national emblem of the United States?

A Probably chosen for its large size and super strength, the bald eagle is the national emblem of the United States. It is not really bald but looks that way because the white feathers on its head, which grow only when the bird is four years old, contrast with its dark body.

White head feathers

Eagle has excellent eyesight

Large, powerful wings for soaring and diving

Toes have long, sharp talons to grasp prey

Q Which bird makes a journey every year from the top of the world to the bottom, and back again?

Male Arctic tern brings his mate fish during courtship

A The Arctic tern makes the longest migration in the world. Flying from pole to pole it migrates about 22,000 miles (35,500 km) a year. The tern spends the short Arctic summer breeding and feeding on insects and fish. It then flies south toward the South Pole for another summer near the Antarctic.

The poles are among the coldest places on Earth

North Pole

South Pole

Identify these wild animals

Can you name the animal shown in each box? There is also a question to answer about each animal, which may help you identify it.

1 What does this animal lick up with its long sticky tongue?

2 The young of these mammals are called leverets. What are the adult males and females known as?

3 In a matter of minutes what can this reptile change about the way it looks?

4 What kind of surroundings does this brightly colored tropical fish live in?

5 Why does this animal have wide, flat feet?

6 This marsupial lives in Australia. What does it do to avoid the heat of the day?

7 Where does this large South American bird build its nest?

8 All 22 kinds of this animal live on which island off the east coast of Africa?

Guess the animal from the part

TAILS

Can you guess which creatures these tails belong to? Two of the creatures live in the sea, one is a member of the same group of animals as spiders, and the others are all mammals.

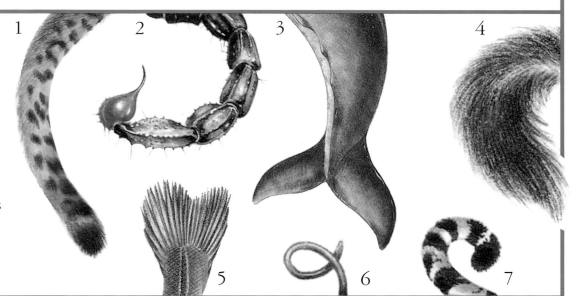

SKINS AND FURS

Some skins are scaly, others are bumpy. Lots of animals have fur, which often has a special pattern. Do you know which animals these skins cover?

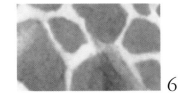

LEGS

Animal legs are all different. Some are made to make long leaps, to run fast, or to walk on sand. Others are adapted for life in or by water. Can you guess which creatures these legs belong to?

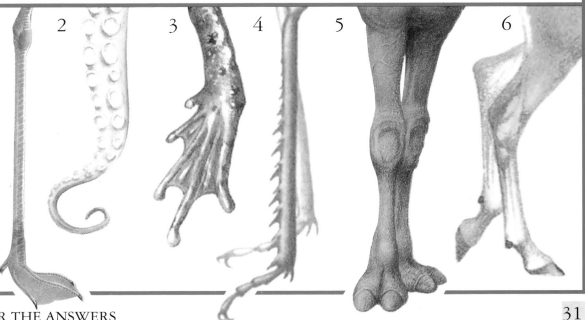

TURN TO PAGE 65 FOR THE ANSWERS

Creepy crawly facts

Q How does the deadly black widow spider get its name?

A This shiny, black-bodied spider is so called because, after mating, the female sometimes eats the smaller male spider. The female is also one of the few spiders that can kill people. Her body is no bigger than a pea, but her bite contains poison that is 15 times more deadly than the poison of a rattlesnake.

Q Which insect uses a sticklike disguise to hide from its predators?

A With a body that looks like a dried-up leaf, the spiny stick insect blends in perfectly with the prickles and curly leaves on which it perches. It moves slowly and sways as it walks, so that it looks like part of the tree moving in the wind.

The legs look like the veins of dead leaves

Sharp spines are like the thorns on the twigs

Body is brownish yellow, like the leaves

Two pairs of legs on each segment

Millipede

Q What is the difference between a centipede and a millipede?

Two legs on each segment

Centipede

A The centipede has one pair of legs on each body segment. It is an active hunter and can run swiftly after insects and other small prey. The millipede does not need to be as quick on its feet because it feeds on decaying plant matter. It has two pairs of legs on each segment. The legs move in waves, pushing it slowly through the soil.

Q When would you see a stag beetle using its huge, antlerlike jaws?

A Only the male stag beetle has such large mandibles (jaws). In fact they are so heavy that they cannot give a strong bite. Instead they are used mainly for show. Just like real stags, males use their "antlers" to threaten and wrestle with other males during the breeding season, to compete for a female.

Large jaw

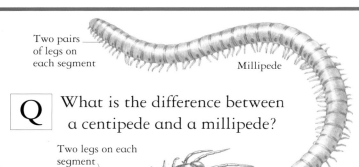

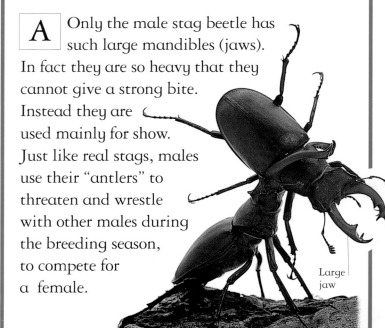

Attack and defense

Q Is the frilled lizard of Australia really as fierce as it looks?

A This lizard is quite harmless. The "frill" is a large flap of loose skin around its neck. When the lizard is startled by a predator, it opens its mouth wide. This makes the frill, which is usually folded flat, open to show a huge ruffle-like collar. If this display does not scare off the enemy, the lizard runs away.

Frill stands up to frighten away the enemy

Q How and why does a Venus's-flytrap plant catch insects?

A This plant has two kidney-shaped lobes at the tip of its leaves. The lobes are hinged at the midrib. When an insect lands on the leaf, it touches sensitive bristles, which trigger the lobes to snap shut. Once trapped inside, the insect is eaten — it is digested and absorbed by glands on the leaf.

Teeth along the edge form a cage around the insect

Trigger bristles

Damselfly lands on the lobe

Q How does the crested porcupine defend itself from an enemy?

Quills, or stiff spines, protect the body

Tail quills are barbed like arrows

A When the crested porcupine feels endangered it rattles the quills, or hollow spines, on its tail to warn predators to stay away. Attackers who come too close are struck with the tail. The sharp quills come out easily and stick into the enemy like arrows.

Q Which sea creatures confuse their enemies by hiding behind a cloud of ink?

A Squids, octopuses, and cuttlefish have an ink gland attached to their digestive system. If they are threatened they squirt a dark-colored ink, called sepia, out of a syphon at the end of their digestive tract. The ink forms a cloud in the water, which confuses the enemy about which shape to follow.

Cloud is like an underwater smokescreen

Common squid

Match the animal to its diet

All the creatures in this box live in the wild. Can you pair each one with the animal or plant (in the box beneath) that it eats in its natural habitat?

Spot the one that does not belong

In each of these boxes two of the three objects have something in common. Can you spot the picture that does not belong with the others, and say why?

FUNGI

1

2

3

BIRDS

1

2

3

REPTILES

1

2

3

TREES

1

2

3

BUGS

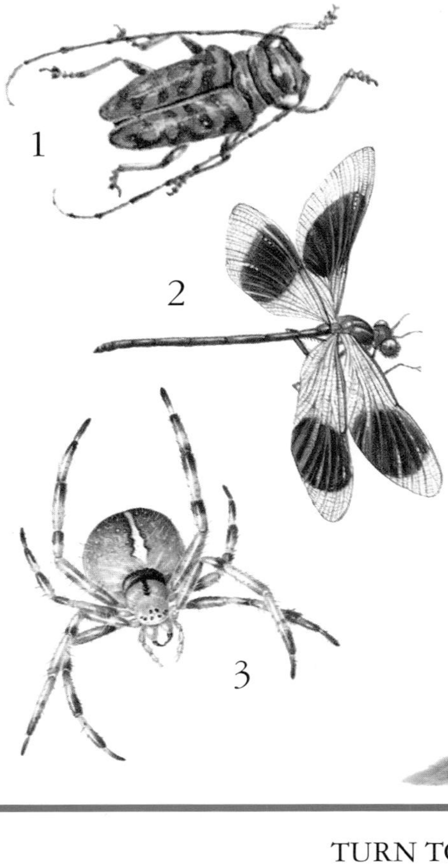

1

2

3

ANIMALS

1

2

3

TURN TO PAGE 65 FOR THE ANSWERS

Test yourself on history

1 A ruthless dynasty ruled China between 221 BC and 206 BC. What was its name?

Army officers in chariots

2 North American colonists issued which famous declaration on July 4, 1776?

William I

3 What is the Domesday Book, and why was it written?

4 Who were the Samurai, and where did they rule?

5 Which general rode into battle on a wild horse called Bucephalus? *Bucephalus was a beautiful horse*

6 In AD 79, what terrible disaster overtook Pompeii?

Disaster strikes Pompeii

7 Sailors used an astrolabe to help them navigate. When and where was it developed?

8 The Phoenicians produced purple color to dye cloth. How did they make it? *Phoenicians dyeing cloth*

9 Books were first made by the Egyptians 5,000 years ago. What did they use to make the paper?

10 Who led the first expeditions to the South Pole, and what happened to the party of British explorers? *Husky-drawn sled*

11 Which sea battle stopped the French invading Britain in 1805?

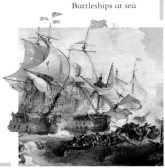
Battleships at sea

12 What was the original name for World War I?

13 Who did the Sioux fight at the Battle of Little Bighorn in 1876, and who won? *Sioux, a North American Indian tribe*

14 Which religious movement was begun with Martin Luther's list of 95 complaints?

Luther pins up his list

15 Between 1788 and 1868, who was sent to Botany Bay?

16 Harappa and Mohenjo-Daro were the world's first cities. Who built them?

17 Why were the Huns, and other tribes that attacked the Roman Empire, called "barbarians"?

18 What happened to the Jews during World War II? *Rounding up the Jews*

19 The ancient Egyptians mummified their dead. Why did they do this, how were the bodies preserved? *Richly d... contains a...*

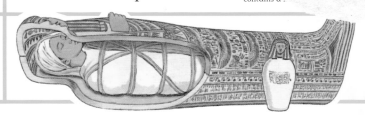

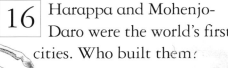

Test yourself on history

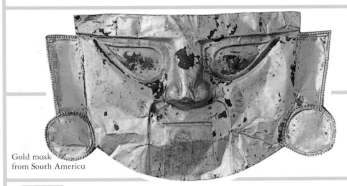
Gold mask from South America

28 In 1963, which American made a now-famous speech that included the words: "I have a dream"?

29 Why did the Pilgrims sail across the Atlantic to North America in 1620?

The *Mayflower*, the Pilgrims' ship

20 In the early 16th century, Spanish adventurers went to South America. What were they looking for?

Coronation of Charlemagne

30 In about AD 60, who led Britons in a revolt against the Romans?

21 Why did the explorer James Cook make his crew eat fresh fruit and pickled cabbage?
James Cook

31 Which empire did Charlemagne rule from Christmas Day 800?

22 The treasure that pirates stole from ships included "pieces of eight." What were they?

Pirate's flag

32 The breastplate and gauntlet are pieces of armor. What parts of the body do they protect?

23 The word "spartan" means strict or brave. Who were the Spartans, why were they famous, and where did they live?

33 This eagle crest belonged to a great family. What was their name?
Black double-headed eagle crest

24 What happened on Wall Street in 1929, causing worldwide economic depression?
Stock market ticker tape

34 The Assyrians ruled in the Middle East 3,000 years ago. Name their capital city.

25 The Vikings sailed to many countries in long-ships. Where did they come from?

El Cid

35 El Cid is a Spanish national hero. How did he become famous, and what was his real name?

26 A knight in full armor had his face [covered]. What did he wear [so] people could identify him?

36 In about 1550 BC, what devastated the Minoan civilization?

27 Amerigo Vespucci was an Italian explorer. Which continent is named after him?

Amerigo Vespucci

37 The tomb of which Egyptian boy-king was uncovered in 1922?

Scarab beetle brooch from the tomb

TURN TO PAGES 40 AND 41 FOR THE ANSWERS 37

Answers for history quiz

1 The Ch'in dynasty from which China gets its name. The dynasty's emperor was Shih Huang Ti. His vast army united the country, which had previously consisted of many warring states.

Paul Revere warns colonists that the British army is coming

2 The Declaration of Independence. Each year on July 4, Americans celebrate the day when the colonists, who were fighting the British over lack of representation in the British government, declared independence.

3 The Domesday Book is a remarkable document. Commissioned by King William I in 1085, it was a detailed survey of the lands, people, animals, and other goods of all the villages in England.

The original Domesday Book can still be seen in London, England

Samurai

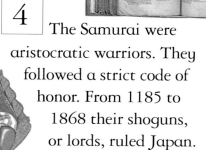

4 The Samurai were aristocratic warriors. They followed a strict code of honor. From 1185 to 1868 their shoguns, or lords, ruled Japan.

5 Alexander the Great (356-323 BC). The brilliant general and his horse were devoted to each other. When the animal died, Alexander built a city in India in its honor.

6 One summer afternoon in AD 79, Mount Vesuvius in Italy erupted. Burning ash from the volcano completely buried the Roman city of Pompeii and its inhabitants.

A plaster cast of the hollow left in the ash by a body

7 The astrolabe was developed during the 8th century by astronomers in Egypt. In 971, the world's first university was founded in Cairo, Egypt, and the Arabs made great advances in astronomy, mathematics, and medical science.

Moorish astrolabe

8 The Phoenicians were Mediterranean sailors and traders. They made the expensive, vivid purple dye from crushed murex seashells. Only high government officials could afford to wear purple cloth.

9 The Egyptians pressed together strands of papyrus reed to form scrolls to write on. Later, the Romans wrote on treated animal skin called parchment. The Chinese invented the paper we use about 2,000 years ago.

Papyrus reeds

10 Captain Robert Scott led the British expedition that reached the South Pole on January 17, 1912. But they were beaten to the pole by Norwegian Roald Amundsen and his team. Only five of Scott's team of ten men reached the pole; unfortunately Scott and the rest of his team died on the return journey.

Answers for history quiz

11 In 1805 the French emperor Napoleon Bonaparte was poised to invade England. But the British fleet under Horatio Nelson destroyed the combined French and Spanish fleet at the Battle of Trafalgar.

Planes were first used in World War I

12 In 1914 a terrible war engulfed Europe. It was called the Great War because fighting eventually took place on every continent. When World War II began in 1939, the Great War became known as World War I.

13 The Sioux fought the U.S. cavalry at Little Bighorn, Montana. The warriors wiped out the cavalry, but the American Indians were eventually forced onto reservations.

Sioux hunting buffalo

14 Martin Luther thought the Catholic Church was corrupt. His list of complaints inspired a mass movement for the reform of the Catholic Church, called the Reformation. Expelled from the Church in 1521, Luther founded Protestantism.

15 Lying south of Sydney, Botany Bay was where James Cook first landed in Australia. From 1788 to 1868 the British sent convicts to Botany Bay to relieve over-crowding in British prisons.

British convicts

Beautiful stone carving

16 In about 2500 BC a great civilization flourished around the Indus River in southern Asia. The people of the region were highly skilled. They built the world's first cities: Mohenjo-Daro in what is now Pakistan, and Harappa, in modern India.

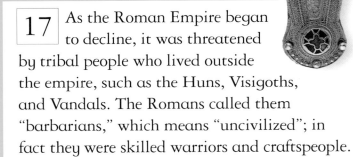

Gold buckle set with garnet

Gold and enameled cloak fastener

17 As the Roman Empire began to decline, it was threatened by tribal people who lived outside the empire, such as the Huns, Visigoths, and Vandals. The Romans called them "barbarians," which means "uncivilized"; in fact they were skilled warriors and craftspeople.

18 In Nazi Germany, Jews were persecuted and imprisoned. By 1945, about six million Jews had been rounded up and murdered in specially built concentration camps. The slaughter of Jews during World War II is called the Holocaust.

Jews were forced to wear a yellow star

19 The Egyptians believed in life after death. They therefore preserved the bodies of the dead as mummies. The internal organs were removed, and the body was then treated to prevent decay.

Answers for history quiz

20 The Spanish soldiers, known as conquistadors, were looking for gold, silver, and land. Two of the most famous conquistadors were Hernando Cortes and Francisco Pizarro.

Cortes, Spanish conqueror

21 Many sailors used to suffer from the disease scurvy, which is caused by a lack of vitamin C. James Cook was an enlightened captain. When he sailed to Australia, Cook kept his crew healthy by insisting that they eat fresh fruit and pickled cabbage.

22 The currency stolen by pirates was doubloons, or "pieces of eight." A doubloon was a Spanish gold dollar that was worth eight Spanish gold escudos.

Gold doubloon

23 The Spartans were the inhabitants of Sparta, the second major city-state of ancient Greece. They were renowned throughout Greece for their courage and discipline. Male Spartans began military training at the age of seven, and remained soldiers until they were 60.

Spartan hoplites (foot soldiers) were very fierce

24 On October 24, 1929, the New York Stock Exchange, on Wall Street, crashed. Stock prices fell, the economy of the country collapsed, and millions lost their jobs. The effects were felt across the world throughout the 1930s.

25 The Vikings were seafarers from Norway, Sweden, and Denmark. They sailed magnificent longships, and settled in many lands, reaching North America in around AD 1000.

Viking longship

26 A knight in armor could be recognized by his coat of arms. The "arms" consisted of two elements – the field (background color or pattern), and charge (symbol or picture).

The coats of arms were displayed on shields

27 In 1499, Amerigo Vespucci became the first European to explore the coast of Brazil. His maps of the New World were so good that sailors referred to the newly found continent as "Amerigo's Land" and it is now known as South America.

United States' flag

28 The influential civil rights leader, Martin Luther King, Jr., made a speech including these words when he led 250,000 people to Washington to demand equal rights for black Americans. In 1964-65, equal rights laws were passed. King was assassinated in 1968.

Martin Luther King, Jr.

Answers for history quiz

29 The Puritans, or Pilgrims, sailed from England to North America in a small ship, the *Mayflower*. The 102 settlers on board were seeking freedom of worship in the New World.

Puritan families lived simple lives, following the teachings of the Bible

30 After Britain had been invaded and conquered by the Romans, the warrior-queen Boudicca led the Iceni tribe in a fierce revolt. But they were no match for the Romans and were brutally crushed.

Boudicca leads her warriors

31 Charlemagne, king of the Franks (the ancestors of today's French) was crowned emperor of the Romans at St. Peter's Basilica in Rome. He created the first important empire in western Europe after the fall of Rome. (It later became the Holy Roman Empire.)

Knight in armor

32 The breastplate of a suit of armor protected the chest. It was flared so that sword strokes bounced off. The gauntlet protected the hand, and was made of many small pieces, which allowed the hand to move freely.

33 Hapsburg (or Habsburg). By the 1500s, this family dominated central and southern Europe, including Italy and Spain. The Hapsburgs ruled the Holy Roman Empire until they were overthrown in 1918.

18th-century Hapsburgs

34 Nineveh was the capital of the Assyrian Empire. The Assyrians were famed for their strength in battle, but their empire collapsed when Nineveh was destroyed by the Babylonians and Medes in 612 BC.

Statues guarded buildings

35 El Cid, from the Arabic word "sidi" meaning lord, was a Spanish nobleman, Rodrigo Diaz de Vivar. In 1094, he recaptured Valencia from the ruling Muslim Moors of North Africa, who had invaded Spain in AD 711.

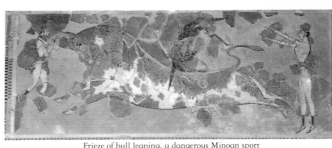

Frieze of bull leaping, a dangerous Minoan sport

36 The Minoans were seafarers who settled on Crete about 4,000 years ago. They built huge palaces and had a rich culture. In about 1550 BC, a volcanic eruption destroyed their civilization. Early this century archaeologists uncovered a Minoan palace at Knossos.

37 Tutankhamen's. He was a boy-king who ruled Egypt some 3,500 years ago. The British archaeologist, Howard Carter, found the boy's tomb, which contained his body and many treasures, in the Valley of the Kings.

Tutankhamen's coffin

Historical events

The dead were carried away on carts and buried in large graves

Q What killed approximately one third of the people in Europe at the end of the Middle Ages?

A In 1347, a terrible disease from Asia swept across Europe. The people who caught it developed black patches on their bodies and usually died within a few days. The plague became known as the Black Death because of the dark patches. Today we know that it was bubonic plague, which was spread by fleas that lived on infected black rats.

Gold nugget

Q Why did people rush to California in 1849?

A The first gold fields were discovered in northern California in January 1848. The following year, many thousands flocked to the region hoping to make their fortunes from prospecting (looking) for gold. It was the greatest gold rush in American history. In 1849 alone, the state's population soared from 20,000 to over 100,000 people.

Prospector sifts for gold

Q Who believed that they had to offer human hearts to their sun god Huitzilopochtli?

Jade mask

A From the 13th to the 16th centuries, the Mexican valley was dominated by the Aztecs. They founded a great empire and captured many prisoners. Believing that the world would come to an end unless they sacrificed people to their sun god, the Aztecs built temples where priests offered the hearts of as many as 1,000 prisoners every week to Huitzilopochtli.

Sacrificial knife

Stone blade

Q Which Chinese army has stood guard for more than 2,000 years?

A Standing in rows, a magnificent army of over 8,000 terra-cotta clay figures watches over the tomb of the first emperor of all China, Shih Huang Ti. Made in 210 BC, the life-size models are exact copies of the army that had helped the emperor unite the rival kingdoms of China.

Some 700,000 slaves and craftspeople made the hollow figures

People in history

Q Which French heroine heard the "voices of angels"?

A In 1429 the French army, led by Joan of Arc, finally defeated the English, who had ruled much of France for the past 100 years. Joan of Arc was very religious, and claimed that she had heard the voices of angels and saints telling her to restore the rightful king of France to his throne.

Joan of Arc led French troops to victory at Orleans

Q In 1492 the Italian sailor Christopher Columbus set sail in search of a new sea route to India. What did he find?

A After sailing westward from Spain for two months Columbus sighted land, which he believed was India. In fact, it was an island in the Caribbean. He was welcomed ashore by native peoples. Since then, these people have been called "Indians" because the explorers thought that they were in India.

Mao Zedong

Q Who led the Long March through China in 1934-5?

A Mao Zedong, head of the Communist Party in China, led about 100,000 people from Kiangshi province, the communist stronghold. They marched to Shensi province in northwest China to avoid attack from the opposition National Party. Only 30,000 people survived the Long March.

The march covered 6,000 miles (9,700 km)

Q How did Charles Darwin shock the world in 1859?

A Charles Darwin was an English naturalist. His book, called *On the Origin of Species*, was published in 1859. In it he put forward his theory of evolution based on natural selection, or "survival of the fittest," and made the then shocking suggestion that humans were descended from apes.

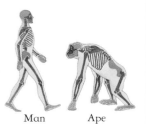

Man   Ape

Darwin shown as a monkey

Name these well-known people

Look carefully at these pictures. Each panel contains portraits of people that are famous for a similar reason. Can you figure out which country they are from, and who they are? The small pictures by the side give you a clue to help you identify them.

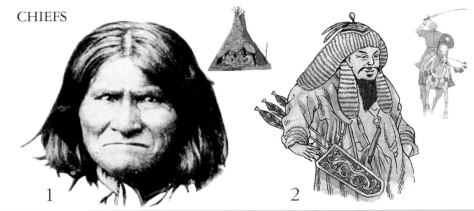

CHIEFS

1

2

RULERS

1

2

3

ARTISTS

1

2

3

MODERN LEADERS

PRESIDENT IS KILLED
Texas Super Escape; Johnson Sworn In

ANC

1

2

3

TURN TO PAGE 66 FOR THE ANSWERS

Make the link and name the event

All the pictures in each of these seven panels are linked either to a war or a revolution. Can you recognize the elements, make the connection, and name the event?

1

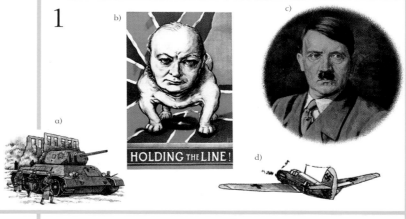

HOLDING THE LINE!

2

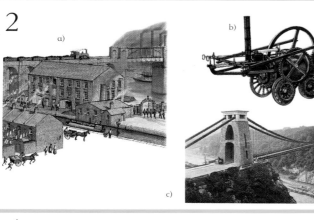

3

4

5

6

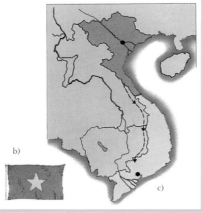

7

TURN TO PAGE 66 FOR THE ANSWERS   45

What people believe

Q What do the gods Ra, Surya, and Apollo have in common?

A People all around the world have told stories abouts gods and goddesses. Although they may have lived far apart and had different cultures, the myths told were often about the same subjects, such as the rain, the sea, the moon, and the sun. Ra from Egypt, Surya in India, and the Greek Apollo were all ancient sun gods.

Greek god Apollo

Indian god Surya

Ancient Egyptian god Ra

Hammer, symbol of the Viking god Thor

Q Who was Thor, and why did he carry a hammer?

A Thor was the Norse god of thunder. The Vikings, warriors and seafarers who lived about 1,000 years ago, believed that Thor controlled the weather. They thought that he rode his chariot across the sky, smashing giant snakes with his hammer and making thunder and lightning.

Thor's hammer was thought to be a thunderbolt

Q Why were 200 people tried in Salem, Massachusetts, in 1692?

A Four hundred years ago, many people believed in witches. They accused old or peculiar women of being in league with the devil, and blamed them for misfortune. During the last big witch hunt, in Salem, 200 women were accused of witchcraft; 19 were hanged.

Q Why was Mother Theresa awarded a Nobel Peace Prize in 1979 ?

A Mother Theresa is a Christian and believes that she has a duty to ease the suffering of the poor and sick. Born in Albania in 1910, she went to India and became a citizen. She founded the Missionaries of Charity, and won the Nobel Peace Prize for her work with the homeless and the dying.

Mother Theresa wearing a flowing dress called a sari

Art through the ages

Clay tablet

Detail of the *Standard of Ur*

Q With what two inventions did the Sumerians of Mesopotamia transform daily life nearly 5,000 years ago?

A During the Bronze Age, the Sumerians developed the system of picture writing known as cuneiform. The pictures were drawn on tablets of damp clay with wedge-shaped pens. They also invented the wheel, which they used on wagons and war chariots, and to make pottery.

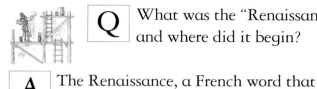

Q What was the "Renaissance" and where did it begin?

A The Renaissance, a French word that means "rebirth," was a period in history that began in Italy in the 15th century. It lasted about 200 years, during which time educated people developed new ideas about the world around them, and rediscovered the arts and learning of ancient Greece and Rome. It produced great artists such as Michelangelo, whose painting on the Sistine Chapel ceiling survives to this day.

Chapel ceiling

Q Which two great composers were born in 1685?

A Johann Sebastian Bach and George Frideric Handel. Both born in Germany, they were great composers of Baroque music – a musical form that dominated the 17th and early 18th centuries. The *Brandenburg Concertos* are among Bach's best-known works; Handel's include *Music for the Royal Fireworks*.

Royal Fireworks

Bach 1685-1750

Q Which musical insects gave 1960's rock music its distinctive sound?

A The Beatles. The band consisted of John Lennon, Paul McCartney, Ringo Starr, and George Harrison, all from Liverpool, England. The Beatles were probably the most influential band in the history of rock music.

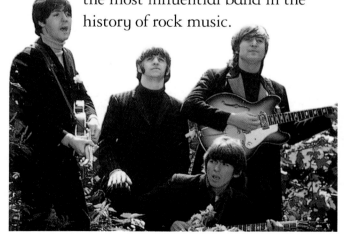

Put the pictures in date order

Look at the pictures in each of these six boxes. Can you say who or what they are, and put them in the correct date order? Begin with the one that lived or was built the longest time ago.

FLIGHT

1

2

3

THEATER

1

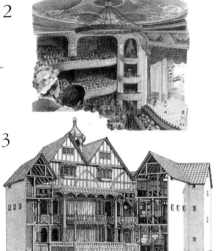

2

3

CASTLES

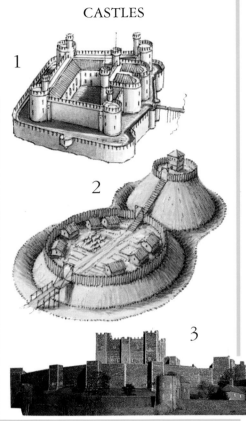

1

2

3

SHIPS

1

2

3

WRITERS

1

2

3

CITIES

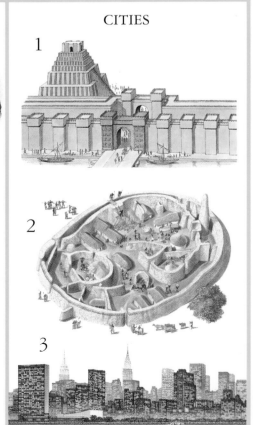

1

2

3

Match the art to the people

All the objects of art in this panel belong to a definite period of history or a certain group of people. Can you match the art to its origins, shown in the panel beneath?

TURN TO PAGE 66 FOR THE ANSWERS

Test yourself on science

Hole in
ozone layer

1 What is the scale that is used to measure the loudness of sound called?

2 Why is the ozone layer surrounding the Earth so important?

3 A jet of boiling water that suddenly shoots up from the ground is called a geyser. When does a geyser blow?

4 What did the scientist Galileo suggest could be controlled by the swing of a suspended weight?

5 When you are very cold, you shiver and get goose bumps on your skin. Why?

Shivering

6 The moon has no light of its own. Why is it then that it can be seen shining brightly in the night sky?

7 There is only one kind of rock that can float on water. What is it called, and why is it so light?

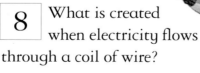
Harrier

8 What is created when electricity flows through a coil of wire?

9 Why are store items marked with panels of black and white stripes?

Eastman

10 In 1888, what did George Eastman invent?

Shoes in
white
light

11 What color would a pair of red shoes appear in blue light?

12 Why do the names of many plastics begin with the word "poly"?

13 What sort of picture will a camera that registers infrared rays take, and what information will be given by the picture?

14 A communication satellite is held in orbit by gravity. How long does it take to orbit the Earth?

Fractal
pattern

15 This pattern is called a fractal. What produces it, and why is it never-ending?

16 Why do astronauts have to wear a special space suit when they venture outside their spacecraft?

17 What is the longest road system in the world called, how long is it, and where is the longest stretch?

18 What is so special about a *Harrier* jump jet?

19 A nuclear power station produces energy from the nuclear fission of uranium atoms. What is fission?

20 Many bicycles have gears. When does a cyclist choose the lowest gear?

Racing
cyclist

Test yourself on science

21 The word "radar" stands for RAdio Detecting And Ranging. How can a radar scanner be used to check car speeds?

22 What is a sextant and who used such a device?

Sextant

23 A cyclist relies on the friction created by the brakes to stop. What is friction?

24 Which woman revolutionized nursing and the care of the sick in hospitals during the 19th century?

25 In the world of computers, what do the technical terms "hardware" and "software" mean?

26 What world-shaking events are measured on the Richter Scale?

27 Where would you find chromosomes, and what do they do?

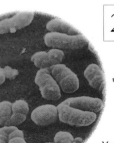
Magnified chromosomes

28 What is the name of the wave that might be produced if there is an earthquake on the ocean floor?

29 Which do you think will hit the ground first when dropped – an egg or a stone of the same size and shape?

Chemical symbol

30 What familiar substance does the chemical symbol H_2O stand for?

31 How much of the air is made up of the gas oxygen?

32 What type of lens is used in a magnifying glass?

Straw appears bigger under magnifying glass

33 Which was the first aircraft to fly faster than the speed of sound, and when did it first do so?

34 Optics, acoustics, and statics are all branches of the same science. What is this science called?

35 Why is the kind of wildlife different at the top and bottom of a mountain?

Baby

36 Medicine has many different branches. What is the name of the branch that specializes in the care of children?

37 Where would you expect to find a crust, a mantle, and an inner and outer core?

38 Contour lines appear on some maps. What do they show?

39 What did Gugliemo Marconi invent?

Marconi

TURN TO PAGES 54 AND 55 FOR THE ANSWERS

Answers for science quiz

1 The loudness of a sound depends on the amount of energy sound waves carry. It is measured on a logarithmic scale, the Decibel Scale. This means each time ten decibels is added to the level, the loudness is multiplied by ten.

Megaphone amplifies sound

6 The moon shines because it reflects light, like a mirror, from the sun. As the moon orbits the Earth, different shapes, or phases, appear depending on how much of the sunlit side of the moon you can see.

The moon appears to grow (wax) and shrink (wane)

2 Ozone forms a layer in the Earth's atmosphere that shields the Earth from the sun's dangerous ultraviolet rays. Too much ultraviolet can harm the nucleus in the cells of plants and animals.

Hole in the ozone layer over the Antarctic lets in harmful rays

7 Pumice, a unique rock that is peppered with tiny holes. It is formed when volcanic lava froth, containing bubbles of gas, hardens. Pumice stone is rough and some people use it to scrub their skin.

Gray pumice stone

3 Deep underground, hot rock can heat water in chambers. When the water boils, the steam increases the pressure and the water is blasted up and forced out in a boiling fountain.

Geyser with a boiling fountain

8 The current in the coil makes a magnet, called an electromagnet, with a field that can be switched on and off. The electromagnet can be made stronger by winding the wire around a piece of iron.

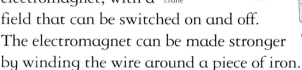

Electromagnetic crane

Coil with iron core

4 At the end of the 16th century Galileo noticed that a suspended weight, or pendulum, moved back and forth regularly. He suggested that this swing could be used to control a clock.

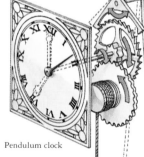

Pendulum clock

9 These striped labels on many items are known as bar codes. The bar code identifies the item and contains other computerized information about it, such as its price. A scanner with semiconductor laser is used to read the code.

Bar code scanner

5 Shivering is the body's automatic way of making the muscles move to produce heat. The bumps appear on your skin because tiny muscles lift your body hairs upright. The erect hairs help trap air close to the skin and so conserve heat.

Erect hair

Goose bump

10 George Eastman invented the handy Kodak camera and the roll film to go in it. His inventions replaced glass plates and bulky cameras, and made photography easy for millions of people.

Brownie box camera

Answers for science quiz

11 In ordinary light, the shoes appear red as they reflect red, absorbing all other colors in the light. In blue light, the same shoes look black, because they absorb all the blue light and reflect no red light.

Red shoes look black

12 Plastics have names like polyethylene, polystyrene, and polyvinyl chloride (PVC) because they are made from molecules called polymers. The word "poly" means many and all polymer molecules are composed of long chains of atoms.

Molecule of polyethylene

13 A camera that uses infrared rays produces a picture known as a thermogram. All objects give out invisible infrared rays. The hotter an object the stronger the infrared rays produced. A thermogram shows the heat of different parts of the object.

Heat picure

14 A communication satellite takes 24 hours to orbit the Earth. It appears to stay stationary over the same part of the globe all the time, so it can receive and send signals. This kind of orbit is called geostationary.

Geostationary orbit

15 The fractal is made by a supercomputer. It is infinite because an equally intricate pattern is made no matter how often a part of the pattern is enlarged.

Powerful super-computer

16 In space there is no air and it is extremely cold. The pressurized space suit provides the astronaut with air to breathe. Without the suit the astronaut would explode. The suit also protects the body from harmful radiation and the cold.

Astronaut in a space suit

17 Covering a distance of at least 29,000 miles (47,000 km), the Pan-American Highway holds the world record. The longest stretch of the road runs from Alaska to Chile, with a small gap in Panama and Colombia.

Route of Pan-American Highway

18 The *Harrier* jump jet is one of few aircraft able to take off and land vertically. The powerful jet nozzles can be rotated downward so that the plane can fly vertically. This means it does not need a long runway, so it can take off and land in confined spaces, such as on a ship.

19 Normally, nothing can enter the nucleus of an atom because it is surrounded by circling electrons. However, if high-speed particles, called neutrons, are fired at atoms of uranium, the nuclei are split. This splitting, which produces heat, is known as fission.

Uranium atoms are split

20 The lowest gear is the one with the largest cog. It is selected to climb hills because it turns the wheel of the bicycle more slowly but with more force. The cyclist has to pedal faster but the extra force makes climbing easier.

A large cog turns the wheel slowly

Answers for science quiz

21 The scanner bounces radio waves off the car. The movement of the car makes the return waves shorter, and from the change in wavelength, the car's speed can be calculated.

Radar speed trap

22 The sextant was used by early surveyors and navigators. It can measure the angle between two distant objects, such as two stars. From the angle, they could calculate their position or find their way.

23 Friction is a force that opposes motion. It is created when two surfaces, such as a brake pad and wheel, rub against each other. Friction, which produces heat and wastes energy, slows down the bicycle wheel.

Brakes rely on friction

24 The woman known as "the lady with the lamp" is Florence Nightingale. After nursing soldiers in the Crimean War, she opened a school in London, England, to improve the standards of nursing.

Nurse Florence Nightingale

25 Hardware is the computer equipment and includes the central processing unit, keyboard, monitor, and printer. The software describes the instructions or programs the computer uses.

Computer harware

26 The Richter Scale measures the force of earthquakes. The scale runs from 0-9, each number marking a force ten times greater than that of the previous number.

Shock waves radiate from epicenter, or focus, of earthquake

27 Chromosomes are miscroscopic thread-like structures made up of genes. They are found in the nuclei of cells and they carry genetic information. Sex is determined by the chromosomes X and Y. A female has two Xs; a male has an X and a Y.

Genes control your looks

28 A tsunami. This huge wave, often wrongly described as a tidal wave, can be 250 ft (76 m) high when it reaches land. When it crashes onto the shore it may cause great destruction. A tsunami can also be caused by a volcanic eruption.

29 The two objects will fall at the same rate and hit the ground at the same time. Falling is controlled by the force of gravity. Gravity is affected by the object's mass (the amount of material in it) rather than the heaviness of the object.

Egg and rock fall together

30 H_2O stands for water. It is chemists' shorthand meaning that each molecule of water contains two atoms of the gas hydrogen (H) combined with one atom of the gas oxygen (O). All chemical elements have a shorthand symbol.

Answers for science quiz

31 Oxygen accounts for 21 percent of air. Nothing can burn without oxygen and it is needed by our bodies to make energy from food. Most of the air – 76 percent – is nitrogen gas. Argon forms 1 percent. The rest is tiny amounts of carbon dioxide, helium, methane, hydrogen, krypton, neon, ozone, and xenon.

Water is sucked up from the saucer into the jar, taking the place of the oxygen in the air that has been burned by the candle

32
Convex lens
A magnifying glass has a convex lens, which is thicker in the middle than at the edges. It magnifies the image by bending the light rays that pass through it so that they come together at a point (focus) after they have passed through the lens.

33 Flown by American pilot Chuck Yeager on October 14, 1947, the rocket-powered *Bell X-1* was the first aircraft to break the sound barrier. A sonic boom is produced when an aircraft flies faster than the speed of sound.

Bell X-1

34 Physics, which is the science of energy and matter. Optics is concerned with the physics of light; the study of sound and how it travels is known as acoustics; statics is the study of the forces that support structures.

A loud sound can make a glass vibrate so strongly that it shatters

35 As you climb a high mountain the temperature drops. It is much colder nearer the top, so only animals and plants adapted to a cold climate can survive.

No trees grow on the peak

36 The branch of medicine dealing with the care of children is called pediatrics. It comes from a Greek word meaning boy or child. It takes years of study to become an expert in a single area of medicine such as pediatrics.

37 The crust, mantle, and core are the layers that make up the Earth. The core at the middle of the Earth is made up of an outer core of liquid iron and an inner ball of solid iron and nickel.

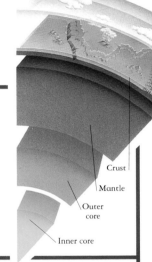
Crust
Mantle
Outer core
Inner core

38 Contour lines on a map connect points that are of equal height above or below sea level. They indicate how the land slopes and show the position of hills and valleys. They are the brown lines on the map shown here.

Map showing contour lines

39 Italian electronic engineer Guglielmo Marconi (1874-1937) invented the first radio system in 1895. Six years later he sent a radio signal across the Atlantic. Today radio waves carry many kinds of information.

Radio receiver

Universal facts

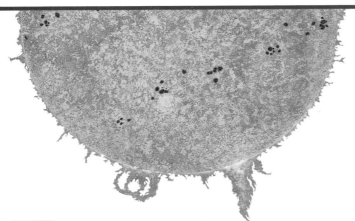

Q The sun's surrounding atmosphere, the corona, emits solar wind. What is this wind and how does it affect the Earth?

A Solar wind is made up of electrically charged particles. The Earth is protected from the wind by its magnetic field, which is pushed into a teardrop shape as the charged particles flow past.

Q What is a star made of, and how does it come into being?

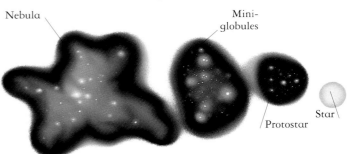

Nebula

Mini-globules

Protostar

Star

A A star is a ball of burning gas. It is born out of a huge cloud of hydrogen gas and dust particles, called a nebula. Gravity pulls some of the dust and gas into a spinning globule, which gradually splits into many smaller mini-globules. Each of these eventually becomes a protostar, and then a star, as its center compresses, heats up, and starts to shine.

Q How is carbon dioxide contributing to the warming of our globe?

A The glass in a greenhouse allows heat from the sun to come in. The glass traps some of the heat when the air outside cools down. The Earth's atmosphere works like the glass. Pollution in the air, such as the gas carbon dioxide, makes the atmosphere trap even more heat, causing the planet to get warmer. Too much carbon dioxide may change our climate.

Escaping heat

Sun's rays

Trapped heat

Q Who first understood the force of gravity, and what is it?

A The famous English scientist Isaac Newton started thinking about gravity in 1666 when he saw an apple falling from a tree. Gravity is a force in every object that pulls things toward it. The heavier the object, the stronger its gravity. Newton went on to prove that the moon is kept in orbit by the Earth's gravity.

The world of weather

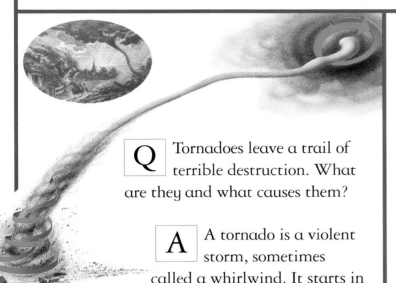

Q Tornadoes leave a trail of terrible destruction. What are they and what causes them?

A A tornado is a violent storm, sometimes called a whirlwind. It starts in a thundercloud. High winds streaming over the cloud set a column of rising warm air spinning. More air rushes into the swirling column to replace the rising air. Like a spiraling funnel coming down from the cloud, the tornado sucks up dirt and other objects off the ground.

Q A weather forecaster can predict the day's weather using a chart. What does the chart show?

Low pressure storm

A The word "high" shows an area of high atmospheric pressure, indicating settled weather. The word "low" shows an area of low pressure, meaning windy, wet weather. The lines around the words are isobars that connect regions of equal pressure. The blue triangles show a cold front; the red semicircles, a warm front.

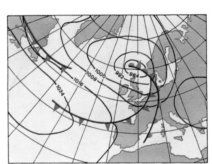

Weather chart

Q How does a glacier change the shape of the landscape it flows through?

A The snow that falls on the tops of high mountains never melts. It builds up in hollows and the lower layers turn to ice. This ice then flows very slowly down the mountain like a river. As it flows, this river, or glacier, grinds away at the landscape to form valleys. Moraine, or rocks, carried in the flow, build up to make walls, behind which lakes form.

Deep U-shaped valley carved out by glacier

Lake forms behind moraines

Q What might you see when it is both sunny and raining at the same time?

A You may see a rainbow if you look toward rain, with the sun shining from behind you. This is because the raindrops reflect the sun's light back to you. Each drop acts like a miniature prism, splitting ordinary white light into a band of colors.

Match the items to their raw material

The same main raw material is used to produce all the items in each numbered box. The raw materials are shown in the center box. Can you figure out which items come from which raw material?

1

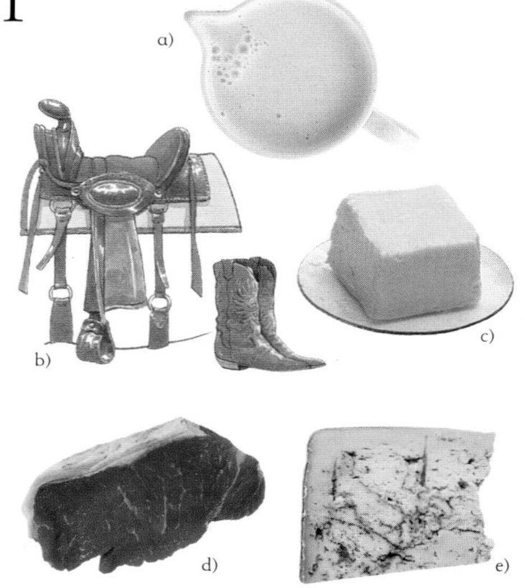
a)
b)
c)
d)
e)

2

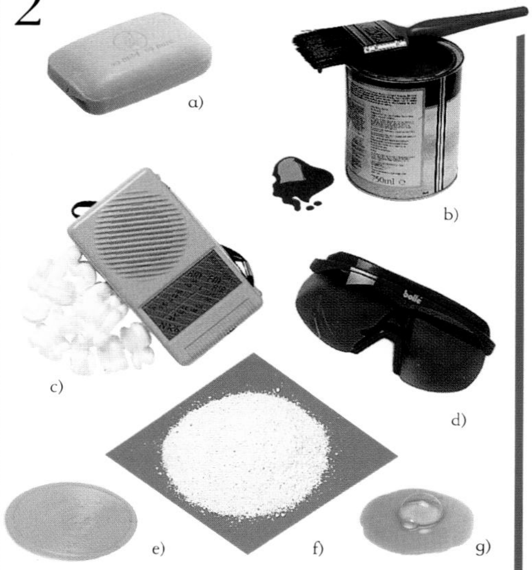
a)
b)
c)
d)
e)
f)
g)

3

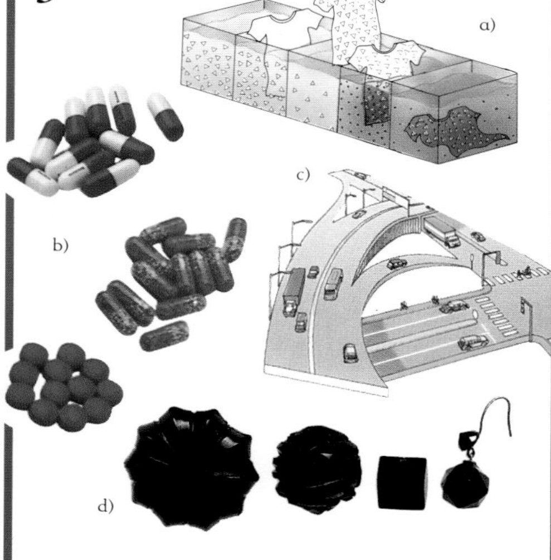
a)
b)
c)
d)

RAW MATERIALS

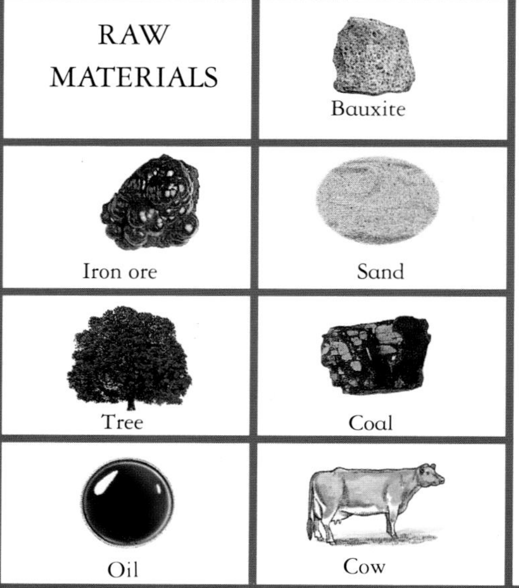
Bauxite
Iron ore
Sand
Tree
Coal
Oil
Cow

4

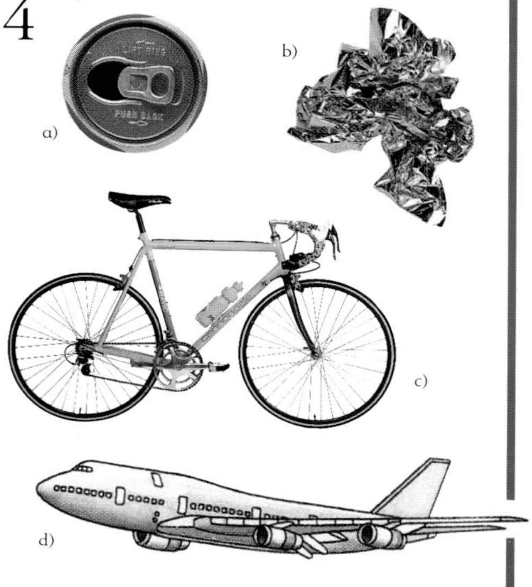
a)
b)
c)
d)

5

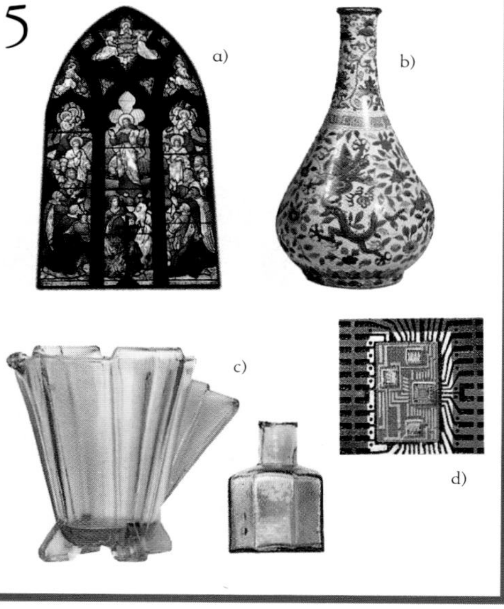
a)
b)
c)
d)

6

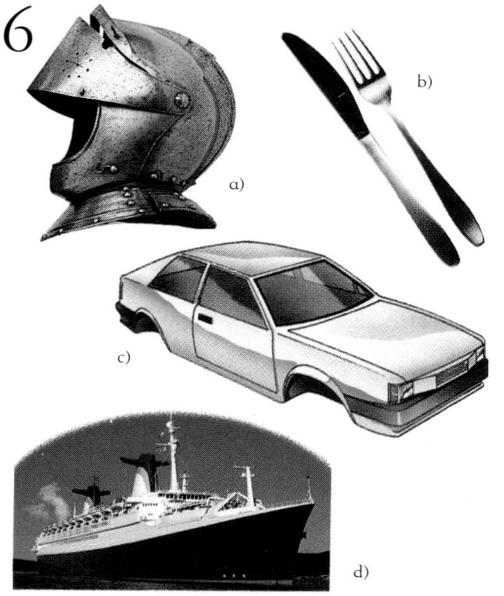
a)
b)
c)
d)

7

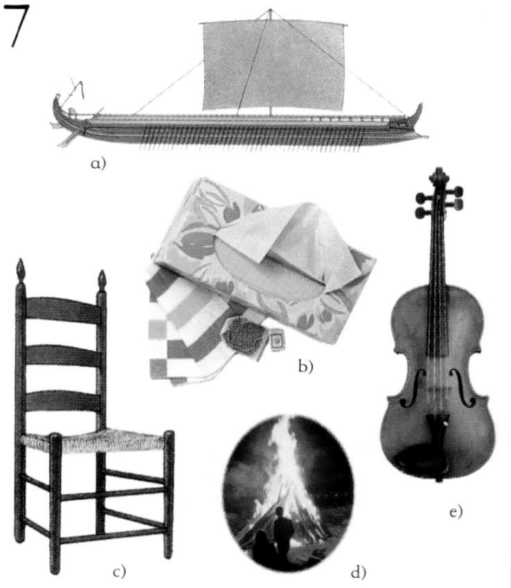
a)
b)
c)
d)
e)

 TURN TO PAGE 67 FOR THE ANSWERS

Find the misfit

All but one of the pictures
in each of these six boxes are
connected in some way. Can
you find the link, and name
the object that does not fit
with the others?

POWER

1

2

3

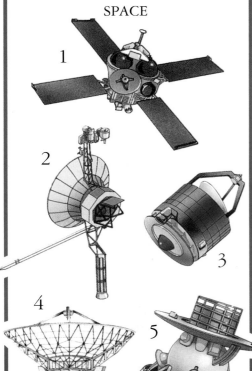

MEASURING

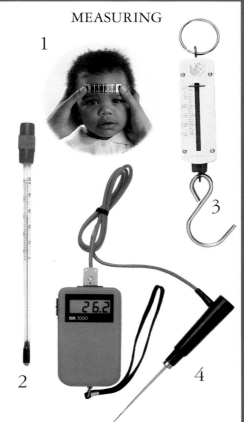

1

2

3

4

EXPLORATION

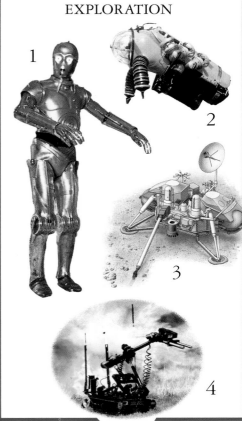

1

2

3

4

SPACE

1

2

3

4

5

RECORDING

1

2

3

4

THE UNIVERSE

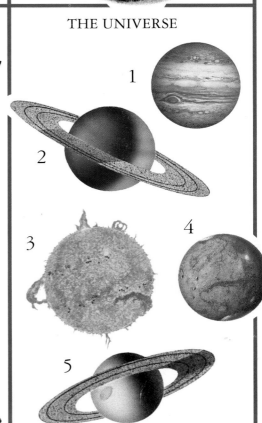

1

2

3

4

5

TURN TO PAGE 67 FOR THE ANSWERS

Famous inventions

Q What invention enabled speech to be sent along wires?

Bell's box telephone

A Alexander Graham Bell sent the first message, "Mr. Watson, come here. I want you," by telephone in 1876. Bell, a Scottish-born American teacher of the deaf, became interested in the way in which sounds are produced by vibrations in the air. He discovered how to transmit the human voice while trying to improve the telegraph.

Alexander Graham Bell (1847-1922)

Thomas Edison (1847-1931)

Q Which two men invented the electric light bulb?

A Thomas Alva Edison in the US and Joseph Swan in England. Working independently, they each demonstrated their first lamps in the same year. Edison began producing lamps for sale in 1880. After Edison unsuccessfully sued Swan, the two men formed a joint company to make bulbs in Britain.

Early electric light bulb

Frank Whittle

Q Which English engineer and pilot suggested the idea of the jet engine?

A Frank Whittle had the original idea for the jet engine in 1928. The first jet-powered flight was made during the 1930s in Germany, but it was not until 1941 that Whittle's engine powered an experimental aircraft in Britain.

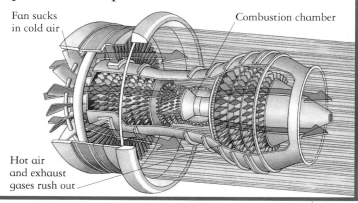

Fan sucks in cold air

Combustion chamber

Hot air and exhaust gases rush out

Metal type

Movable type arranged on composing stick

Grip

Q Who produced the first printed book in Europe?

A In the 1400s Johannes Gutenberg, from Mainz, Germany, invented a printing press. He developed movable type by casting metal in molds to form individual letters, and adapted a wine press to make a printing press. One of the first books he printed was the Bible. The Chinese began printing with wooden blocks in AD 868.

Great discoveries

Q Who discovered X rays in 1895, and why were they given this strange name?

X-ray photograph

Microsurgery

A X rays, like light and radio waves, are a type of radiation. They were first identified by the German scientist Wilhelm Roentgen. The letter X is a symbol for the unknown. Roentgen called the rays X rays because he did not understand what they were. Today X rays have many uses. In medicine they can be used to look inside the body without using surgery.

Q Francis Crick and James Watson worked out the structure of deoxyribonucleic acid (DNA) in 1953. What is DNA?

Model of DNA showing double helix structure

Chemical link

A DNA is found in the nucleus, or control center, of almost every cell. It is a long molecule that has a double helix (spiral) structure. Chemical "bridges" link the two strands of the helix. The genetic code of the cell, which is like a recipe for what the cell does and how it works, is determined by the sequence of the chemical bridges.

Q What is so special about the Hubble Space Telescope?

Hubble Space Telescope

A Launched in 1990, the Hubble Space Telescope is an optical telescope that flies 310 miles (500 km) up in the sky, in an orbit beyond the Earth's atmosphere. In this position, it avoids the blurring effect of the Earth's atmosphere and can collect much clearer images than telescopes on the ground.

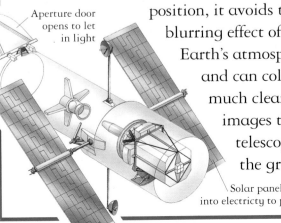

Aperture door opens to let in light

Solar panels turn sunlight into electricty to power telescope

Q Who discovered how blood circulates around the body?

A In 1628, an English doctor named William Harvey (1578-1657) put forward his theory of circulation. He found that blood constantly circulates around the body in arteries and veins. He showed that the heart pumped the blood and that valves in the veins stopped the blood from flowing backward. He drew detailed diagrams to explain his theory.

William Harvey

Diagram showing circulation in the arm

Pair the device to the image it makes

All these components, instruments, or machines are used to produce a different kind of image. Can you match them to the pictures in the panel below?

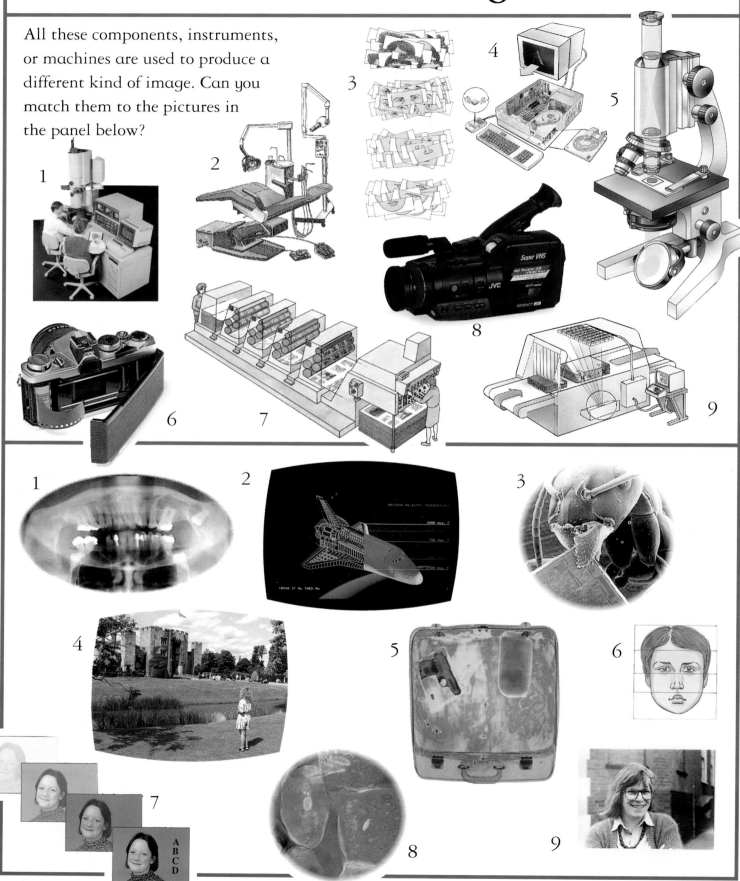

Put the body part in the correct place

The boxes around the girl show a body part and ask a question. Can you identify the part, put it in the correct place on the girl's body (marked with a letter), and answer the question?

1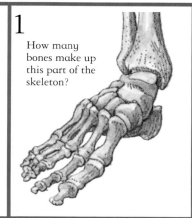
How many bones make up this part of the skeleton?

2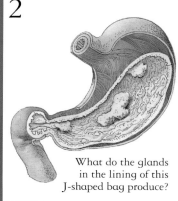
What do the glands in the lining of this J-shaped bag produce?

3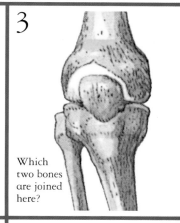
Which two bones are joined here?

4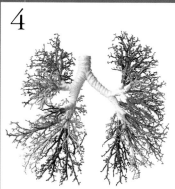
Which gas do we need to live?

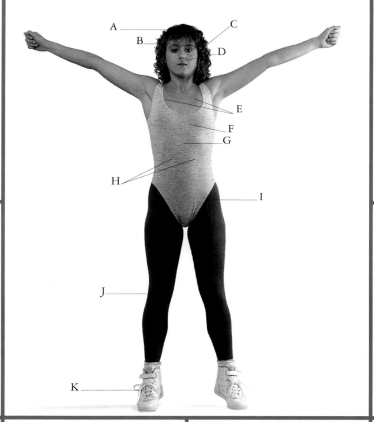

A
B
C
D
E
F
G
H
I
J
K

5
Can you name the hole that lets light into this structure?

6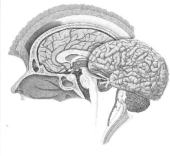
What is the name given to an automatic reaction that we make without thinking?

7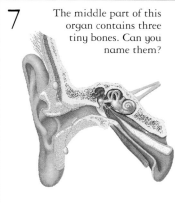
The middle part of this organ contains three tiny bones. Can you name them?

8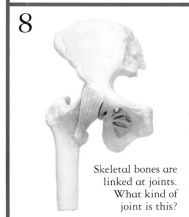
Skeletal bones are linked at joints. What kind of joint is this?

9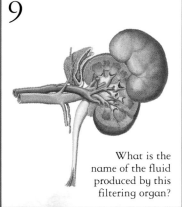
What is the name of the fluid produced by this filtering organ?

10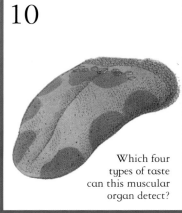
Which four types of taste can this muscular organ detect?

11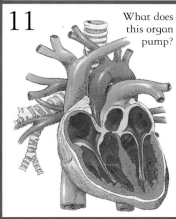
What does this organ pump?

TURN TO PAGE 67 FOR THE ANSWERS   63

People and places puzzle answers

Page 16   Guess the flags

 1. Olympic flag

 2. Italy

 3. United States of America

 4. Japan

 5. Israel

 6. India

 7. United Kingdom

 8. Brazil

 9. Canada

 10. United Nations

 11. France

 12. European Union

 13. Australia

 14. Race car finish flag (checkered flag)

Page 17   Name the countries and continents

1. Australia
a) Tropic of Capricorn
b) Sydney

2. Africa
a) Nile River
b) Equator

3. India and subcontinent
a) Himalayas
b) Sri Lanka

4. South America
a) Amazon River
b) Andes Mountains

5. United States of America
a) New York
b) Grand Canyon

6. United Kingdom
a) North Sea
b) London

7. Japan
a) Pacific Ocean
b) Tokyo

8. New Zealand
a) Auckland
b) North Island and South Island

Page 20   Name these famous buildings

ANCIENT BUILDINGS
1. Golden Temple, Amritsar, India.

2. The Pyramids, Giza, Egypt.

3. The Parthenon, Athens, Greece.

MODERN BUILDINGS
1. Toronto Sky Dome Stadium in Canada is used for sports and entertainment.

2. Sydney Opera House in Australia is an arts center for theater, opera, concerts, and exhibitions.

3. The Guggenheim Museum in New York City houses modern and contemporary art.

TALL STRUCTURES
1. Statue of Liberty, New York City, NY, US 305 ft (93 m) including the pedestal and base.

2. Empire State Building, New York City, NY, US 1,250 ft (381 m).

3. Eiffel Tower, Paris, France, 1,051 ft (320 m).

4. Big Ben, Houses of Parliment clock tower, London, United Kingdom, 316 ft (96 m).

5. Canadian National Tower, Toronto, Canada, 1,815 ft (553 m): the tallest of these six buildings.

6. Leaning Tower of Pisa, Italy, 179 ft (55 m).

Page 21   Find the picture that does not belong

ARTISTS
2. *Madam Gachet in the Garden*, painting by post-impressionist Vincent van Gogh; *The Dance at the Moulin Galette* by Pierre Auguste Renoir (1) and *The Butterfly Chase* by Berthe Morisot (3) are both impressionist paintings.

MUSICAL INSTRUMENTS
2. The soprano saxophone is a wind instrument; the cornet (1) and the French horn (3) are both brass instruments.

FLAGS
1. The flag of the United Nations is the flag of an organization; the semaphore flag for the letter X (2), and the signal flag for the word "do" (3) are both flags used to send messages.

SPORTS
2. The runner competes in the summer Olympic Games; skiing (1), ski jumping (3), and ice hockey (4) are all sports included in the separate Winter Games.

UNIFORMS
3. The ceremonial soldiers' uniform of the US; the others are naval uniforms of China (1), Russia (2), and United Kingdom (4).

BUILDINGS
3. Alcázar castle, Spain; The Blue Mosque, Turkey – Islam (1), Hindu Temple, India (2), and St. Peter's Church, Vatican City, Rome – ... (4), are all places of worship.

Nature puzzle answers

Page 30   Identify these wild animals

1. Giant anteater.
It eats ants and termites.

2. Hare.
The males are called
jacks, the females are jills.

3. Jackson's chameleon.
It changes the color and pattern of
its skin to match its surroundings.

4. Angelfish.
It lives around coral reefs.

5. Bactrian or Asian camel.
Its wide feet splay out to keep the
camel from sinking into soft sand.

6. Wombat.
They shelter from the hot sun
in their underground burrows.

7. Toucan.
This bird nests in a hole in a tree.

8. Ring-tailed lemur.
All lemurs come from Madagascar,
the large island off Africa.

Page 31   Guess the animal from the part

TAILS

1. Snow leopard

2. Scorpion

3. Sperm whale

4. Skunk

5. Fang tooth fish

6. Pig

7. Tiger

SKINS AND FURS

1. Rattlesnake

2. Gila monster (lizard)

3. Zebra

4. Tiger

5. Nile crocodile

6. Giraffe

LEGS

1. Flamingo

2. Octopus

3. Frog

4. Grasshopper

5. Dromedary or Arabian camel

6. Fallow deer

Page 34   Match the animal to its diet

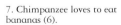

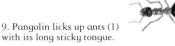

1. Rhinoceros grazes on
grass (2).

2. Giant panda eats bamboo (8).

3. Bumblebee feeds on nectar
from flowers (3).

4. Archer fish spits drops of water on bugs,
such as spiders (4), and then eats them
when they fall into the water.

5. Songthrush eats
snails (5).

6. Grizzly bear scoops
salmon from rivers (9).

7. Chimpanzee loves to eat
bananas (6).

8. Lions are carnivores and eat
large prey, such as zebra (7).

9. Pangolin licks up ants (1)
with its long sticky tongue.

Page 35   Spot the one that does not belong

FUNGI
2. Fly agaric toadstool is poisonous;
the chanterelle mushroom (1) and
the field mushroom (3) are both edible.

BIRDS
3. The kiwi cannot fly;
the Canadian goose (1) and
the tawny owl (2) can both fly.

REPTILES
2. The marine turtle lives
in the sea; the Chilean
tortoise (1) and the
hinge-back tortoise (3)
both live on land.

TREES
2. Scotch pine is a coniferous (evergreen) tree; the
plane tree (1) and the rowan or mountain ash (3) are
both deciduous trees: they lose their leaves in winter.

BUGS
3. The spider is an arachnid and has eight legs;
the long-horned beetle (1) and the damselfly (2)
are both insects, which have 6 legs.

ANIMALS
3. The dog is alive today; the
woolly mammoth (1) and the
dodo (2) are both extinct species.

History puzzle answers

Page 44 Name these well-known people

CHIEFS

1. Geronimo, Chiricahua Apache Indian chief of North America, 1829-1909.

2. Genghis Khan, creator and leader of the Mongol Empire of northeastern Asia, 1162-1227.

RULERS

1. Louis XIV, King of France, ruled 1643-1715.

2. Tutankhamen, Egyptian pharaoh who ruled Egypt 3,500 years ago.

3. Elizabeth I, queen of England for 45 years, ruled 1558-1603.

ARTISTS

1. Elvis Presley, American "king" of rock and roll, 1935-1977.

2. Ludwig van Beethoven, German composer, 1770-1827.

3. Anna Pavlova, Russian ballerina, 1881-1931. Her most famous solo was *Dying Swan*.

MODERN LEADERS

1. John F. Kennedy, youngest American president, born 1917, assassinated 1963.

2. Mohandas Gandhi, who instigated India's independence from British rule, 1869-1948.

3. Nelson Mandela, born 1918, leader of the African National Congress against apartheid in South Africa, is still alive today.

Page 45 Make the link and name the event

1. WORLD WAR II
a) Russian T-34 tank used in 1943 tank battle b) Adolf Hitler, leader of the Nazi party c) Winston Churchill, British war-time Prime Minister, depicted as a British bulldog on a poster d) Messerschmitt fighter plane flown by the Luftwaffe – the German air force.

2. INDUSTRIAL REVOLUTION
a) Clifton suspension bridge, designed by Isambard Kingdom Brunel (1806-1859) b) Factory town c) Early steam locomotive, built by Richard Trevithick, ran on rails for the first time in 1801.

3. RUSSIAN REVOLUTION
a) Vladimir Lenin, Russian leader and founder of the Bolshevik party b) Russia's last Czar, Nicholas II and his family c) Communist red star with hammer and sickle.

4. FRENCH REVOLUTION
a) Napoleon Bonaparte (1769-1821) led military takeover in 1799 to end French Revolution b) Execution of Louis XVI in 1793 c) Sans-culottes (without trousers), name given to revolutionaries who wore simple clothes d) Marianne, imaginary revolutionist shown on Republican stamp.

5. AMERICAN CIVIL WAR
a) Abraham Lincoln, president of the US, who stoped slavery b) Auction of slaves at a slave market c) Soldier of the Confederate army of the southern states, led by General Robert E. Lee d) Union soldier, Union army defeated Confederacy in 1865.

6. VIETNAM WAR
a) Vietnamese jungle was bombed with chemicals to strip the leaves off the trees by US Air Force b) Vietnam flag c) Map of war zone, showing North and South Vietnam.

7. CHRISTIAN CRUSADES
a) Knights hospitallers looked after hospitals on route of warring pilgrimage to Palestine b) Siege weapons c) Sultan Saladin (1137-93), leader of the Muslim forces d) Richard the Lionheart, king of England from 1189 to 1199, took part in the Third Crusade.

Page 48 Put the pictures in date order

FLIGHT
1. Montgolfier balloon, made first flight with passengers in 1783. 2. Otto Lilenthal hang glider 1890. 3. Concorde, supersonic jet, broke the sound barrier in 1970.

ENTERTAINMENT
1. Delphi amphitheater, 5th century.
2. Globe theater, 16th century.
3. Victorian playhouse, 19th century.

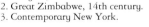

CASTLES
1. Wooden motte (hill) and bailey (court), 6th century. 2. Norman stone castle, 11th-13th century. 3. Spanish round tower castle, 16th century.

EXPLORERS
1. Viking ship, 9th century.
2. Capt. James Cook's ship *Endeavour*, 1768.
3. Deep sea bathyscape *Trieste*, 1960.

WRITERS
1. Shakespeare, playwright (1564-1616). 2. Karl Marx, German philosopher and writer (1818-83). 3. Anne Frank, young war diarist (1929-45).

CITIES
1. Babylon, 2000-600 BC
2. Great Zimbabwe, 14th century.
3. Contemporary New York.

Page 49 Match the art to the people

1. Louis XIV chair and French gentleman of same period (1).

2. Aboriginal dreamtime painting and Aboriginal people (3).

3. Carved wooden totem pole and American Indian (5).

4. Norman Bayeux tapestry and Norman soldiers (7).

5. Celtic engraved bowl and Celtic people (9).

6. Carved ivory snow knife and Inuit (8).

7. Greek vase and ancient Greek person (4).

8. Medieval illuminated manuscript and monks of the Middle Ages (6).

9. Egyptian hieroglyphs and ancient Egyptian scribes (2).

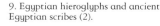

Science puzzle answers

Page 58　Match the items to their raw material

1. a) milk, b) leather goods, c) butter, d) beef, and e) cheese are all products from the COW

2. a) soap, b) paint, c) polystyrene and plastics, d) polycarbonates, e) shampoo, f) powdered soap, and g) dishwashing liquid are produced from OIL

3. a) dyes, b) drugs, c) coal tar-pitch for road surfacing, and d) jet jewel are all made from COAL

4. a) aluminum can, b) foil, c) bicycle frame, and d) aircraft body are all made from aluminum, extracted by the Bayer process from BAUXITE

5. a) window glass, b) porcelain, c) glassware, and d) silicon chips all have the same raw material — SAND

6. a) iron armor, b) stainless steel cutlery, c) low-carbon-steel car body, and d) medium-carbon-steel ship body are all smelted from IRON ORE

7. a) ship, b) paper products, c) furniture, d) wood for fuel, and e) wooden musical instruments are all products from the TREE

Page 59　Find the misfit

POWER
2. The coal-fired power station uses non-renewable fossil fuel; solar panels (1), and wind turbines (3) are both forms of renewable energy.

MEASURING
3. Spring balance measures weight; mercury thermometer (1), fever strip thermometer (2), and digital celsius thermometer (4) are all used for measuring temperature.

EXPLORATION
2. Atmospheric diving suit for a diver to explore at very deep depths; anthropoid robot C3PO (1), space probe robot (3), and bomb disposal robot (4) are all types of robots.

SPACE
4. Dish-shaped radio wave antenna; *Mariner 9* (USA) (1), *Voyager 1* (USA) (2), *Giotto* (European Space Agency) (3), and *Venera 9* (USSR) (5) are all space probes.

RECORDING
4. Barograph used to measure and record air pressure; pocket watch (1), exceptionally accurate atomic clock (2), and stopwatch (3) all record or measure time.

THE UNIVERSE
3. Sun is a star; Jupiter (1), Saturn (2), Earth (4), and Neptune (5) are all planets.

Page 62　Pair the device to the image it makes

1. A scanning electron microscope magnifies the whole object, such as an ant shown at 15 times its size (3).

2. The dental X-ray machine takes X-ray pictures such as a dental X ray (1).

3. Photofit cards are put together to make photofit picture (6).

4. A computer can be used to generate a graphic of a space shuttle (2).

5. The light microscope magnifies objects normally invisible to the naked eye, such as human cheek cells magnified 200 times (8).

6. A 35mm single lens reflex camera uses film, which can be processed to produce a photographic print (9).

7. A four-color printing press will combine magenta, cyan, yellow, and black to produce a full-color printed image (7).

8. The video camera records video film, which can be viewed on your television screen (4).

9. The baggage scanner, a type of X-ray machine, where the monitor screen shows an image of the contents of a suitcase for security purposes (5).

Page 63　Put the body part in the correct place

1. The foot is located at K
26 bones, including those of the ankle.

2. The stomach is located at G
The glands in the lining of this J-shaped bag produce acid and digestive juices.

3. The knee joint is located at J
Thighbone (femur) and shinbones (tibia and fibia).

4. The lungs are located at E
Oxygen.

5. The eye is located at B
The pupil.

6. The brain is located at A
A reflex.

7. The ear is located at C
Anvil (incus), hammer (malleus), and stirrup (stapes).

8. The hip joint is located at I
Ball-and-socket joint, which allows bones to swing in two directions and also to twist.

9. The kidneys are located at H
Urine, which is then stored in the bladder.

10. The tongue is located at D
Sweet, salty, sour, and bitter flavors.

11. The heart is located at F
Blood.

Index

Index

Picture credits

Picture research: Charlotte Bush

The publishers are grateful to the following individuals and picture libraries for permission to reproduce their photographs.

Abbreviations: t = top, b = below, c = center, l = left, r = right.

Alvis Ltd: 59cra; The Ancient Art and Architecture Collection: 41cr, 49tl; The Bridgeman Art Library: 44cla/British Museum 39c, 39cr, 47tl/Cairo Museum & Giraudon 37br/Christies, London 58cl/Louvre 49cl/National Maritime Museum 36tr/Private Collection 44cra, 49tcr/Queensland Art Gallery 49tr/Staatliche Museen zu Berlin 49cla/The Vatican 47tr; Bruce Coleman Ltd: Gene Ahrens 15tr/Brian and Cherry Alexander 10tr/Norman Scwartz 52cl/C.B. & D.W. Frith 8bl/Gerald Cubbitt 21bra/David Howton 14br/Michael Kilmec 59tcl, 67tl/John Markham 42clb/Alfred Pasieka 58bcl/Fritz Penzel 20c/Dr. Eckpart Pott 15br/Warner Stoy 36cl/Norman Tolamin 48tc, 66tc; Crown: Public Record Office

(E31) 38cb; C.M.Dixon: 39tc; et Archive: 46tr; Mary Evans Picture Library: 8tr, 9cl, 10tl, 11bc, 12cla, 18cl, 22tr, 25cr, 41ca, 41br, 43br, 44crb, 45tr, 45cra, 45cla, 45clb, 45br, 48br, 48bc, 49bcl, 49crb, 51tl, 51br, 54cb, 60tc, 60br, 61cla, 61cr, 61br, 66tl, 66ca, 66c, 66bc; German National Tourist Office: 12clb; Giraudon: 37cra; Sonia Halliday: 45bcr; Julia Harris: 59cla; Michael Holford: 40cl/British Museum 38cr; Hulton Deutsch: 36bra, 43cl, 44bc, 47br, 48c, 60clb; Hutchison: Sarah Errington 13clb, 13tr; By courtesy of IAL Security Products: 62crb; The Image Bank: 13bl, 15cl, 19cl/P.& G. Bower 21crb, 65br/Joseph B. Bribnoto 58bc/Giamalberto Cigolini 62crb/Gary Cralle 20bcr/David W. Hamilton 48cr/Francisco Hidalgo 37tl/Michael Pasczior 19bl/Harold Sand 42cb/Stockphotos Inc. 52cr/Eric Wheater 9bl; Ann Ronan at Image Select: 60cla; Stephen Kirk: 35tr; The Kobal Collection: 44clb, 59tcr; By courtesy of Kodak: 50bl; Anne Lyons: 58br; The Raymond Mander and Joe Mitcheson Theatre Collection Ltd: 10bl; The Mansell Collection: 47cl; NASA: 57tr, 61clb; Network: Goldwater 13br; Peter Newark's Western Americana: 36ca, 39cl, 42ca, 44tc, 45tc, 45crb, 46bl, 49bl, 49cr, 66crb; The Nobel Foundation:

46cb; Novosti: 45ccr; Ordnance Survey/© Crown Copyright: 55crb; Christine Osborne Pictures: 9tl; Osel Group by courtesy of Quest, Marshall Cavendish: 59tr, 67tr; Philips Scientific: 62cra; Popperfoto: 44bl, 45bl, 46br; Roger Viollett: 43tl; Science Photo Library: Biophoto Associates 51cl/Ken Briggs 59tl/Earth Satellite Corporation 13crb/Simon Fraser 57br /Eric Grave 62bc/Adam Hart-Davis 53c/IBM 62t/NASA 50tl, 52tl/NIBSC 25cl/David Parker 53bc/Royal Greenwich Observatory 59c/Jim Stevenson 62clb/Dr. T. Thompson 61tl; Frank Spooner Pictures: Eric Bouvet/Gamma 44br; Sporting Pictures UK: 21bl, 21clb, 65bl; Syndication International: 44cl; Jerry Young: 34t, 34br, 35tr; Zefa: 19br, 20tl/Dr. David Corke 42cla/Damm 11cbl/W.F. Davidson 38tr, 58clb/K. Goebel 44ca/Heilmann 13cla/Messerschmidt 11bl.

Every effort has been made to trace the copyright holders and we apologize in advance for any unintentional omissions. We would be pleased to insert the appropriate acknowledgment in any subsequent editions of this publication.